Find Your Flavor

A Recipe for Discovering Your Ideal Career

By Lauren Doyle, M.S.

Find Your Flavor
A Recipe for Discovering Your Ideal Career

Published by Getting Results
1290 N Palm Ave.
Sarasota, FL 34236

Copyright © 2021 Lauren M Doyle

All rights reserved. No part of this book may be reproduced, stored in a retrieval system, or transmitted in any form or by any means without the written permission of the publisher. Printed in the United States of America.

ISBN: 978-0-578-31693-2

DISCLAIMER AND/OR LEGAL NOTICES

While the publisher and authors have used their best efforts in preparing this book, they make no representations or warranties with respect to the accuracy or completeness of the contents of this book. The advice and strategies contained herein may not be suitable for your situation. You should consult a professional where appropriate. Neither the publisher nor the authors shall be liable for any loss of profit or any other commercial damages, including but not limited to special, incidental, consequential, or other damages. The purchaser or reader of this publication assumes responsibility for the use of these materials and information. Adherence to all applicable laws and regulations, both advertising and all other aspects of doing business in the United States or any other jurisdiction, is the sole responsibility of the purchaser or reader.

This book is intended to provide accurate information with regard to the subject matter covered. However, the Author and the Publisher accept no responsibility for inaccuracies or omissions, and the Author and Publisher specifically disclaim any liability, loss, or risk, whether personal, financial, or otherwise, that is incurred as a consequence, directly or indirectly, from the use and/or application of any of the contents of this book.

I dedicate this book to the many people who helped forge my path. There have been many, and without one of them, I may be in a very different place. You all contributed to my life by design and each has inspired parts of this book.

Table of Contents

Are You Ordering Off the Kids' Menu? 3

Chapter One:
Why This Will Pay Off 9

Chapter Two:
Things to Do Now: Play. Experiment. Sample. 17

Chapter Three:
Master Your Mind: Who's Pulling Your Strings? 33

Chapter Four:
Know Yourself: What Is Your Operating System? 47

Chapter Five:
The Process: Identifying Your Ingredients 61

Chapter Six:
Creating Your Ultimate Recipe 91

Chapter Seven:
Invest in Yourself: Moving Forward with Confidence 99

Resources: 107

About the Author 111

Are You Ordering Off the Kids' Menu?

"What do you want to be when you grow up?"

When you were five or six years old, I imagine you had a solid handle on your answer. Fireman, ballerina, football player, singer. Most young kids can answer that question in a heartbeat, and the sky's the limit. You were probably no different... back then.

At that age, you weren't tasked with considering the reality of the educational requirements and income potential for your choice. You could simply dream and let your imagination run wild. You could imagine your dream job anyway you wanted and never had to dig into what might be the less pleasant aspects of your career choice. The fireman's always a hero and the 5-year-old doesn't know about the more dangerous and even mundane tasks that are associated with the job. The little girl dreaming to be a singer only thinks about being on stage but not the continual rehearsals or negotiating performance contracts.

But you're not that little kid any more... and career choice is a huge decision with layers of consequence – not the least of which may be a waste of time and money – for making the wrong one. Pile on to that the outside influences coming your way, from parents, mentors, and even peers. It's probably been pretty easy up to this point. From one year to the next, you proceeded through the system, passing from grade to grade and taking the required courses. Pre-algebra, followed by algebra, then trig and calculus. Others were making the big decisions for you. Now you have to plan your own future.

There's a tremendous amount of pressure on young adults today to figure out what they want to do with their lives. Well-meaning adults may prod you, asking where you see yourself in five years when you're struggling to figure out tomorrow. Yeah, you're facing a big decision at a time in your life when things are about as tumultuous as they can get. A big decision when you may not be at all prepared to make it.

My goal in writing this book is to help you understand that there is so much more to career choice than your personality profile and aptitude tests. There are also far more choices than you can imagine. At your age, I struggled with career choice and set my sights on being either a therapist or an attorney. My profile tests would have sent me in either direction. My parents encouraged me to pursue a profession in law and continually told me that I'd be so well-suited for it. Apparently, I excelled at arguing with them. I took one summer to explore one of my options and spent a few months inside a law firm. It undoubtedly helped clarify my decision – it allowed me to see the inner workings of an attorney's life and I wanted no part of it. Therapist it would be.

So, I put myself on that path, knowing that I had a long, long road of post-secondary education ahead of me. But I'd made my choice, set my goals, and persevered. I dedicated eight years to becoming a marriage and family therapist and distinctly remember in the last semester of my graduate program, after all the classes and all the time, sitting in a room and realizing that this was going to be the reality of my choice… and my only thought was, *"This is not what I thought I signed up for!"* Dimmed room, hour after hour, with people crying and depressed, and most appointments scheduled for evening hours when I'm a morning person! I loved working with people but therapy would be too depressing for me.

"*Eight years in and what am I doing? Do I have to start over? How can I do something different?*" I stepped back to reassess. I knew I loved business, so I considered pursuing a Ph.D. in organizational psychology. Another commitment of time and money. As I grappled with my decision, I had the lucky coincidence to have a conversation with the mother of one of my clients. I told her I was thinking about working under the guise of business, since I both loved and was fascinated by it and enjoyed working with the human mind. She told me it sounded similar to a program in which her husband was working and then introduced us. He took me to an event the following weekend, where I met the founder of a coaching company that I ultimately began working for the day after I completed my graduate program. It was a great fit. However, it was somewhat of an accidental coincidence that brought it to fruition.

Upgrade Your Menu

I share my story because it was really the result of taking this ingredient and that ingredient… **and then mixing it with an ingredient I didn't even know existed!** Until I began grappling with a stranger about what I was thinking, I never even knew that being a business coach was "a thing." No one ever told me when I was making my initial career choice that such a thing existed. I had been limited by my own inexperienced view of careers and, frankly, the world.

Throughout this book, I hope to be the "stranger you grapple with" who can help you understand that there is so much more to career choice than what you may have been told. Career counselors are nice in theory, and perhaps, you've met with one. However, no matter how well-meaning they are, they typically have limited exposure to the students with whom they meet. One or two sessions simply cannot provide reasonable clarity about a career choice you will live with for the rest of your life. Personality profiles and aptitude tests may provide a foundation, but they do not shed light on what may be the missing special ingredient that really creates the recipe that is truly right for you. Choosing a career is a complex process that cannot be oversimplified. I hope to broaden your perspective so that you won't have to rely on a coincidental accident.

I liken it to having to select from the kids' menu. Think about going out to dinner with your parents when you were younger. No matter where you went, the kids' menu was always the same: chicken fingers, hot dog, pizza, mac and cheese, hamburger… with a side of french fries or fruit. That was it. Rarely any variation and nary a creative concoction. I appreciate that the kids' menu serves a purpose and know that young kids can be picky eaters and usually enjoy what's on that menu.

That was fine back then. It's a lot like the 5-year-old making the career choice – limited by what they think they know about the world and what they think they'll like to do. When it comes to career choices, the kids' menu typically includes doctor, attorney, teacher, IT specialist, maybe sales representative.

In answering the question, "What do you want to be when you grow up?" most only consider the career *title*, even if that title happens to extend beyond the typical "doctor, attorney, teacher," etc. Only considering the title is like saying, "I want chicken"... yet there are so many different and great ways to prepare and enjoy chicken! The various dishes are driven by the elements of the recipe: actual ingredients, marination, cooking temperature and time, and even **when** to add various ingredients to take it from plain ol' chicken to something delectable.

I doubt you are satisfied any longer with being limited to the kids' menu in a restaurant, and I want to help open your eyes to the expansive list of richer ingredients that you can combine to create the career that will allow you to design and really live the life you want.

Are You Ordering Off the Kids' Menu?

Chapter One:
Why This Will Pay Off

Now more than ever, it's critical to gain clarity about "what you want to be when you grow up," and I assure you, although it's a factor, your age is only a small part of the equation. Enter the escalating cost of higher education. Every day you can read an article, blog, tweet, or social media post about some aspect of tuition – from reining in the cost to the impact of student loans on the lives of graduates that are affecting them into their 30s and even well beyond.

Current culture seems to place a stamp of approval on using college years to "find yourself." There is no shortage of students who select the school *first*, then decide what they want to study rather than the other way around. With that approach, clearly the choice is driven by something other than class offerings or noted reputation in a particular area of study. Perhaps it's location, a legacy decision (if relatives are alumni), or school reputation – whether that be academic or athletic.

The number of freshmen who enter as "undecided" and decline to declare a major upon admission is growing. In some instances, parents who were unable (for whatever reason) to attend college, may push hard for their children to do so, regardless of their career aspirations or even whether or not college is the correct post-secondary educational choice.

According to a variety of studies, approximately one-half to three-quarters or more of students change majors in college prior to graduation… at least once! The National

Center for Education Statistics places the number at 80 percent and suggests that the average change of major occurs three times. Another study indicates that six in ten students take longer than four years to earn a bachelor's degree, while 90 percent of them believe they will, in fact, graduate in four years, according to a national study conducted by a research institute at UCLA. The U.S. Department of Education says that one-third change their mind after they've selected a major and ten percent switch majors two *or more* times. Additionally, they report that the average student takes 4.4 years to earn a bachelor's degree from a research university and 4.8 years from all other institutions.

So yeah, now delaying a decision on course of study and/or switching majors certainly seem culturally acceptable. "It's okay to be undecided. It's okay to switch majors. You want to be happy, right? Don't stick with it if you're not enjoying it."

Acceptable but very expensive none the less. According to ValuePenguin, Inc., the average annual total cost of public colleges is $25,290 (in-state) and $40,940 (out-of-state) with private colleges coming in at $50,900 for an average of $39,000. So just a single major change can add a semester or a full year to the time it takes to earn your degree. It also can add nearly $40,000 to your tuition bill. Ouch. Considering that, I hope you are beginning to understand the value of taking time now to do some of the introspective work it takes to determine what it is you want to do – and what will be the right fit – earlier in your educational career.

I'm uncertain if there's a lack of direction in today's age that enables and possibly even encourages this expensive indecision or if previous generations just sucked it up, stuck to their choice, tromped through plugging away in their career for years, and coped with the consequences... as unhappy as they may have been. I coach many of these people as well. They typically reach out once they have reached their 50s, after spending the past 25 to 30 years in their career. They feel unhappy yet are not sure what to do "now" because they have built a lifestyle around their current level of income and "starting over" feels impossible.

Culturally, there may have been greater resilience and endurance in previous generations forced by a lack of social acceptance about using college to "find themselves" and lack of acceptance (and finances) regarding a change in majors. Look back a generation or two and those nagging, seemingly unending student loan payments were not part of the typical landscape.

Regardless of the reason, there certainly has been a cultural shift, and the only outcome to it is that the cost of college goes up even higher. Unless you have a wealthy family that is covering your tuition – no matter how long it takes you to finish, those student loans go up as well right along with the prospect of having to make those payments for years, if not decades, into the future. That financial burden may alter every aspect of your adult life from marriage, to buying your first home, to starting a family.

Evidence supports this unfortunate reality. Millennials' unprecedented student debt reduces their chances of buying a home. According to a 2016 study conducted by Freddie Mac (officially the Federal Home Loan Mortgage Corporation) and Experian, a 10 percent increase in student debt decreased the likelihood of home purchase by four percent, with an even greater problem for those who incurred student loans but failed to finish college. Total debt is a driving factor in the ability to qualify for a mortgage or to obtain one at a more reasonable interest rate. Additionally, more than half the workers employed in the "essential workforce" (e.g., health care, education, law enforcement) have made housing decisions based on student debt. A driving factor is a lack of a down payment or adequate down payment. All of this adds up to an inability to purchase the house you may want in a reasonable neighborhood... and we're talking basics here, so forget about the high-end amenities and fancier locations.

Besides the housing issue, your ability to invest sooner will also be impacted. Of course, you may not be giving much, if any, thought to investing for retirement at this point; however, the math is really, really simple. The sooner you begin, the more time the beauty of compounding interest can work in your favor. Consider the example of Jack, Jill, and Joey as shared by *U.S. News*: Jack starts investing $200 per month in the stock market at age 25. By age 65, his portfolio value is $520,000. Jill waits ten years to begin investing that amount. When she's 65, her portfolio is worth about $245,000 (just over half). And finally, Joey doesn't start investing until he's 45. That same $200 per month investment only yields him $100,000 at age 65, likely delaying his retirement.

The real moral of both of these examples is that it pays to do the extra work now to figure out the best career path for yourself... keeping your student loans in check and avoiding creating a negative financial situation for yourself that will impact you well into adulthood.

More Than Money and Time

You are, indeed, faced with a consequential choice.

Part of the cultural shift is an increasing amount of pressure on students to figure out what they want to do for the rest of their lives. At 18 years old, a student has not been able to have the types of experiences they need to make the best choices. Sure, there is a rare, small percentage who have a clear vision early and follow it for their entire lives with much satisfaction and happiness, but I assure you, it's a very small percentage.

There are plenty of students, notably the Type-A ones, who struggle with incredible anxiety about making the wrong career and course of study decision. Many understand the ramifications of choosing the wrong major or even the wrong school, and it leads to sleepless nights, worry, and stress... at best. It can even lead to some turning to drugs and alcohol, becoming more reliant on substance abuse in an attempt to combat ongoing bouts of depression and self-doubt.

There can be an internalization of an incorrect decision about career planning. *"What's wrong with me? Why can't I get it right?"*

Besides the cost of poor career choice planning in terms of money and time, there is an inadvertent and possibly higher cost that comes with the loss of self-esteem. Perception of self-worth plummets, and there's an insidious, underlying, not-so-nice voice that declares, *"I'm a loser because I can't figure it out."* But how can you figure out what you want out of life when you've had such limited exposure to life in the first place? With unrealistic pressure to "figure it out," many students will start borrowing ideas from others about what they should do or be. Often, it comes from parents; however, peers play a bigger role today, thanks to the impact of social media.

Far too much of a sense of self-worth today comes from the number of likes anyone gets. And yes, it can actually infiltrate all the way to career choice. For some young adults, they don't follow the career that is most suited for them because it doesn't sound cool on social media or it doesn't have the level of prestige in the eyes of their social circles. Unfortunately, I'm not making this up.

The world is a different place today, and social pressures, due in very large part to social media, are at an extreme level – far higher than they've ever been. As a result, there is actually a loss of self-identity or missed identity as teens and young adults try to carve themselves into what they think they're supposed to be based on their "life on social media" rather than determining more effectively who they really are, so they can more accurately determine who they are becoming – not to satisfy social norms and stigmas but to satisfy their own personal appetite of personalized interests.

As an example, I'll share the story of a client I'll call James. James had an interest in Human Resources but never allowed himself to pursue, sample, or even apply to such positions for fear of "not looking cool" to his peers. What could be more ho-hum to share on social media than that? As a result, he started and quit three jobs within 14 months because none of them were a fit for him. He quickly found himself unemployed for the next six months as he tried to cherry pick career opportunities that seemed cool but didn't satisfy his particular appetite. Once he recognized how this was getting in his way and thwarting his own opportunity for happiness and personal success and fulfillment, he opened himself up to the opportunities that truly interested him and as a result has identified the career "staircase" that aligns with his interests and talents. (I will address more about the staircase to your career later in this book.)

I realized I had to write this book when I discovered the benefits of going through the process that I'm about to share with you that go far beyond avoiding excessive tuition expenses and wasting time in the wrong major. I found that when the students I was coaching went through this process, it not only clarified their direction regarding career choices, it really boosted their self-esteem and confidence. In turn, they're less apt to feel insecure about their choices and hopeless about their future. With that increase in confidence, they put less stock in the opinions of their peers and what's shared on social media and become more focused on succeeding in their careers. As a result and possibly most important, they become less susceptible to using substances to get through their day, ultimately avoiding the bouts of depression that are too commonplace with today's youth.

The young clients I work with get so much more out of the process, including how to manage their own thoughts, especially when those thoughts lead to anxiety and/or sadness. They also learn how to negotiate challenges in relationships of all types, and so much more, all based on the fundamental principles that I am going to cover with you in the chapters that follow.

So, it's time for you to stop ordering from the kids' menu and begin experimenting with different ingredients in different ways to create a recipe for your future that you can truly savor. As I guide you through this in the following chapters, you're about to discover that this is going to be so much more than career-path choices and decisions!

Chapter Two:
Things to Do Now: Play. Experiment. Sample.

As I mentioned earlier, thinking only about career title is like ordering "chicken" without specifying how you'd really like that chicken prepared. Don't settle for boring poached chicken or chicken fingers or nuggets when mixing in other ingredients that suit your taste can make it so much better!

In a society that increasingly operates on "now" and "faster," it's like we're trying to microwave everything, including career choice. Yes, you can microwave chicken, but it's likely to turn out bland and boring, especially when no other ingredients are added! The general expectation (and one that you might have right now) is: "I go to college, choose a career, study the subject matter, graduate, get the perfect position in my designated career… making lots of dough."

When any part of this expectation chain is not met, young adults are disappointed and start questioning everything – themselves included. Now you may be antsy to get right to the process – the nuts and bolts, if you will – regarding how to go about determining the career choice that will be the best match and be most fulfilling for you. ***However, I'll caution you that we must first create a solid foundation on which to build or the process won't be effective and might not even make sense to you.***

It's like working out. To get the most out of any sort of workout, it's best to begin with stretching. Sure, plenty of people skip that or don't spend as much time as they should stretching before exercising, but any trainer will tell you that it's really an important part of the process. You'll get more out of the workout, whether it's strength or cardio, and stretching also helps you avoid injury.

So to start, I'll introduce you to the two things you should be doing right now… the latter of which may not seem like it has anything to do with career choice, but I assure you, it's integral to the entire process. Let's start with the easier – and easier to understand – task.

Play. Experiment. Sample

The first of the two jobs you have right now is to play, experiment, and sample. We're always telling young kids to go out and play. In elementary school, there's recess for this very activity. We encourage experimentation and trying different things. That's how kids learn, and we understand that.

But somehow, and I'm not certain the age at which this happens, we stop doing that. Recess is a distant memory by high school, but even as adults, we should never stop "going out to play" at least figuratively if not literally. It seems the more responsible we become, the more we expect to have all the answers. Honestly, I – along with all the adults I know – are still learning every day… still having new experiences. The more we learn, the more we come to realize we'll never have all the answers.

To circle back to the concept of a limited menu, young kids are often happy with the kids' menu because it's what they know and are comfortable with. Let's face it: humans are resistant to change. You may think that chicken fingers with either barbeque or honey mustard sauce is the only way you ever want to eat chicken. Then, perhaps because someone with more experience insists, you take a taste of chicken Marsala, chicken Oscar, or Coq Au Vin and discover that there is, indeed, so much more to chicken than nuggets or fingers. There are new ingredients that combine to be far more delicious and enjoyable. But until you try it, you'll never know. Experiment! Sample!

Having experiences, especially as a result of purposefully playing, experimenting, and sampling, is the only way to learn what does and doesn't suit you. As I shared in my own story, the experience of working in a law firm was so valuable because it clearly showed me that it was ***not*** what I wanted, and it prevented me from heading down the wrong career path, possibly spending three to five years doing what I didn't enjoy rather than a three-month stint in a summer job.

Many times, college kids come home for the summer and either relax and hang out with friends or opt for an easy job that doesn't require much thought and that is completely unrelated to their interests. They've done a lot of studying and thinking in school and feel like they want and need a break. You may be in this boat. I think this is a big mistake and a wasted opportunity to learn more about the different ingredients they (and you) should be playing and experimenting with.

When I work with clients in choosing careers, I have them go back and review *every* experience they've ever had, including things like volunteering, summer jobs, retail work, babysitting, lawn care, etc. I ask them to delineate everything they liked and didn't like about each of those experiences, forcing them to really pick it apart.

As an analogy, it's like working with a sommelier in choosing wine who picks apart the flavors in a glass of wine when they taste it. You might laugh when it's suggested you can taste lead pencil or petroleum in a wine, but the sommelier understands and is an expert in the nuances of flavor… of ingredients based on their vast experiences and study of their craft. But when the average person hasn't had those experiences or education, they will not taste the flavors. They can be limited to thinking red vs. white… much like having chicken without considering all the different ways in which it can be prepared.

Similarly, in going through this exercise with clients, I can uncover a lot about what they like and don't like. Do they like working in a busy, high-energy environment? Or a quiet, reflective one? Working one-on-one or with a bigger team? Indoor or outdoor jobs? Physical vs. mental challenges? Types of ages they like to work with? Even where they work?

Clients can answer the questions based on their previous experiences, but they may not be able to discern how it fits into their career choices, much like a person may not be able to taste "the lead of a pencil" in a glass of wine because it hasn't been pointed out to them.

It's a matter of figuring it out through experimentation and having some help putting all of the pieces together. Too many young adults dismiss what they've learned about themselves through experience because they don't think it relates to their career aspirations and expectations. For example, I worked with a young woman who was majoring in finance, and her summer jobs revolved around babysitting. She didn't see a correlation; she only saw it as a means to earn money. When I prodded further and asked her what her favorite aspects of babysitting were, it turned out that playing outside with the kids was what she most enjoyed rather than being cooped up inside all day. That may seem completely unrelated to a career in finance, but that career is one that is predominantly spent indoors behind a desk without a lot of physical activity, if any. It's a simple example, but it does shed a lot of light on what could turn out to be a total disconnect between her career choice and what she really enjoys.

We spend so much of our lives doing what we do in our careers, yet society historically has segregated career and life. You go to work with one persona and then at the end of the workday and on weekends, you live the rest of your life being who you really are. This mindset builds in a dissatisfaction with careers and work. Only in recent years are we seeing a greater focus placed on "work/life balance." Your career will be a part of who you are. It's all connected, and it *is* life. Those two aspects are inseparable. If you pretend that not to be the case, you are setting yourself up for frustration, anxiety, and unhappiness or even depression.

Another client, I'll call Jill, told me that what she'd learned in her summer job was that she didn't like having a boss tell her what to do. Granted, there are many people who don't "like" that aspect of any position, so we delved further into her experiences to uncover other ingredients. Doing things on her terms needed to be a big part of her "entrée" choice. No matter what she'd done to this point in her various life experiences, including both team sport participation and her sorority, she was always chosen as a leader. That completely aligned with her desire to do things on her own terms – she was accustomed to being the leader!

We needed to incorporate this prevalent ingredient into Jill's future plans and career choice path. Through her summer job experiences, she learned that rote-type, repetitive work was not at all for her. She was always quick to put a creative spin on everything she did. Through our conversations about her experiences, I was able to help her formulate the right recipe that would most likely lead her to the best career choice for her.

As humans, we all tend to "take for granted" who we are. It's like only knowing you have chicken to cook with. While you have many options for recipes (including a greater assortment of ingredients to add), you are still quite limited than if you added fish, steak, tofu, shrimp, scallops, etc. to the menu from which you can choose. Our limited perspective of ourselves is much like only cooking with chicken – it is, well, very limited.

Without someone with whom to have these conversations and provide some guidance, it is difficult to compare and contrast your own experiences and ingredient preferences. This is the core of playing, experimenting, and sampling in reviewing all of your experiences, so you can combine the right ingredients for yourself.

As we go through the process, we'll continue to uncover this, but you first have to truly know yourself, so let's dive into the second of the two things you should begin doing right now, and this brings me to perhaps the most important critical ingredient – your mind. I find that no one teaches kids how to actually manage their thoughts. As you'll see, this is perhaps the greatest skillset anyone can cultivate.

Brain vs. Mind

There are two different aspects to the thing that rests inside your skull between your ears. You have a brain and a you have a mind, and they are not one and the same. The brain is the physical gray matter and the cells and neurons that all contribute to its ability to function and run the entire body, an important job, yes, but only founded in physiology. Conversely, your mind is comprised of your ***thoughts***.

School trains your brain, but it's up to you to train your mind. Training your mind is the second of the two "jobs" you have on your path to choosing the career that is right for you.

I find that the young adults with whom I work are so focused on getting that "career job" that they fail to recognize that they should be working today while they're trying to figure out their path and who they are. So much attention goes into building and developing brains, along with all the knowledge we pack in there, that not enough time – and often no time – is spent on training the mind. It is likely you've never even been told that training your mind is a "thing." It is not only a thing – it is one of the most important things. Having a trained mind, provides an immense advantage.

There can be a lot of anxiety and depression that can come along with this process, and there's a whole host of theories about the drivers behind it, much of which can be attributed to social media. There's no question that the occurrence and extent of anxiety and depression in today's young adults surpasses that of previous generations. I can't say that we're any better or worse regarding the process of developing minds today, but I do believe there is certainly not enough time spent on mind development. The good news is that there does seem to be greater awareness of the subject. The bad news is that there is very little guidance on how to do it. One of the real benefits of developing your mind is to hedge against being unconsciously driven toward a certain career. Additionally, understanding what makes you tick will help you align your career in a way that will be fulfilling to you.

The concept of managing your mind – your thoughts – may be new to you. No one really teaches kids how to manage their thoughts. In fact, many of the adults with whom I work have also never been exposed to this idea. People fail to recognize the distinction between the brain and the mind. The brain is filled with knowledge, information, and experiences. The mind is the interpreter of all that, including the conversation that goes on inside your head about it.

Most don't recognize that you are not your mind. The mind is something to be managed. However, your mind is such an ongoing narrator of life that's been there for as long as we can remember that we buy into the notion that it is somehow "us." We collapse the "me" and the "mind" into a single entity and presume they are the same thing. We also succumb to the notion that anything the mind creates (thoughts about our experiences) is the truth – when in fact, it is often far from the truth, but we buy into it as if it is. Our thoughts then incite our emotions.

Who's Pulling Your Strings?

If you learn to control your mind, you can manage anything. So, so… so many people do not recognize that they are not their mind and that their mind is something they can manage. When you fail to manage your mind and control your thoughts, your mind becomes the puppeteer and you become the puppet with random and unpredictable emotional and behavioral reactions that occur as the direct result of the thoughts flowing through your mind.

As with anything you want to manage, recognition is the critical first step. You cannot solve a problem without first understanding what the problem is. The more clearly you recognize and define the problem, the better your solution will be. You must re-train your mind… your thoughts… to align with what you want. Before we delve into this, I must warn you: It takes work. The best analogy to managing your brain is, again, that of physical fitness. No matter what physical shape you may be in, I'm certain that you understand that one trip the gym, one workout, one brisk walk is not going to get you in top physical condition. The same is true for working out the muscle of your mind. I want you to equate managing your mind with working out your body. Your physical reward for working out is improved health and greater physical ability. Your reward for training your brain is the ability to live the life you want, including a career choice that supports what truly makes you happy.

When I talk about re-training your mind, I'm talking about managing your thoughts and that inner voice in your head… the one you may be confusing with "you." Stop for a moment to consider all of the random thoughts that run through your brain every minute, every hour, every day.

Things to Do Now: Play. Experiment. Sample.

Consider a typical scenario: You jump out of bed, ready to tackle the day with smile and spring in your step. You're on fire. Then you hit that one class with the teacher who perhaps makes a critical comment about the class in general or gives you a lower grade than expected, and the rest of your day derails. Rather than taking this as a single event, your thoughts – that voice in your head – allow it to shape the rest of your day, and that shape is not positive. Your smile is gone and your ambition is deflated all because of thoughts you couldn't manage or control... all because the voice kept rambling on negatively.

That voice, the narrative in your mind, can make you anxious. It can make you think that every teacher is critical of you and all of your hard work has been for nothing. You're going to fail this class... and all your classes. Now you may think this is an over-reaction... and it is! But when it happens to you, your voice starts running that track that you buy into, and your actions, reactions, and emotions are directed as a result.

People tend to equate their thoughts with who they are, and I want you to understand that those two things are not synonymous. You are not your thoughts. You are not the voice in your head. The purpose of learning to manage your mind is to understand how your thoughts can run your emotions... and reactions to events. The more you are able to control the voice and random thoughts, the more effective you become at consciously designing your career choice and your life.

When your reactions are driven by your thoughts, either bad or good, you are the puppet and the outside, uncontrollable forces or people become your puppeteer pulling the strings... that is, if the voice in your head is not managed. Once you start working out your mind, you will have the ability to shift the direction of it on purpose, not just when it happens accidentally from one minute to the next. Managing your thoughts allows you to manage your emotions, which ultimately allows you to manage your actions.

By learning to manage your thoughts and quiet the voice, you can reframe how your mind sees an event. It's just an event, good or bad; however, your thoughts will arise around the event, and your thoughts (good or bad) determine your emotion about it and reaction to it. Your mind will always create thoughts around an event because it needs to. Your mind must fill in gaps and create an understanding of the world. The more effective you become at managing your mind, the greater your ability is to create the end result you want and less likely to be drawn into various, random directions. The key is understanding where your mind went during any event and having the ability to consciously direct it.

A simple event – a comment from a teacher or classmate or a misinterpreted text – can have you in a foul mood because of the uncontrolled thoughts that immediately jump in and take over. Suddenly, you're living the moment, the day, and your entire life at the whim of your thoughts and the voice in your head rather than by the design that you want. The more quickly you notice where your mind went, the faster you can let go of it along with the tension and negative emotions that resulted.

Become the Puppeteer

Most people don't realize how they are a puppet to their random thoughts. My goal is to change you from being the puppet of your thoughts to being the puppeteer – the one controlling the strings and the outcome. Marcus Aurelius said, "Our life is what our thoughts make it." I want to alter this: Your life is what ***you allow*** your thoughts to make it.

This probably seems impossible at first because we don't really think about our thoughts. They just happen, and we don't recognize that we're a puppet to these random thoughts that come and go. You take it as though it is somehow the truth and your emotions follow like a loyal little puppy. However, in the same way that you can manipulate a physical movement, you can manipulate your thoughts. You can manipulate your arm and fingers to reach over and pick up a pencil, and you do that consciously. With training, you can manipulate your thoughts to go where you want them to and make them do what you want. You become the puppeteer. You take charge of pulling the strings to control your thoughts rather than the other way around.

Public speaking is a great example. It is one of the greatest fears that humans possess. Many people actually break out into a sweat, hands start shaking, and voice quivering even at the thought of having to speak in public. That reaction is the result of random, uncontrolled thoughts that irrationally convince you that the audience will hate your message, hate you, and boo you off the stage! This is crazy, yet people who fear public speaking – some even rank it higher on their fear list than fear of death – are ruled by the unconscious and irrational stream of thoughts… thoughts that take over and run the show.

Where do thoughts even come from? When you think about the overwhelming randomness of your thoughts, it seems pretty crazy. Your thoughts are habitual, and like any habit, they can be changed. But like all habits, change takes work. The more you work on your mental muscle, the more you will realize how crazy your thoughts are and how crazy it is to let these random thoughts drive your actions and emotions.

The good news is that you are not permanently sentenced to the randomness of your thoughts. You can take control of the puppet strings, but it does take work. Going back to that fear of public speaking: Some of the greatest orators in history learned to manage their thoughts and train their minds to overcome their fear of public speaking… Thomas Jefferson, Warren Buffet, Joel Olsteen, and even Mahatma Gandhi. Yes, it took work, but they succeeded. So can you.

You don't go to the gym once and expect to be in great shape. Furthermore, once you get in shape, you must continue to exercise to maintain your physical fitness. The same thing is true for your mental fitness.

To start, begin to recognize thoughts as they come up. For example, when that teacher was critical, where did your thoughts go? What thoughts did you have? Are you upset only by the comment or did your mind race out of control from a single criticism to failing every class? Acknowledge that your mind just made that up. There was no basis in reality for the voice in your head suggesting you'd fail everything because of one single criticism. In fact, maybe the teacher was having a really rotten day and simply spoke out of turn.

When thoughts that have no basis in reality pop up, understand where your mind goes by default. Start to take inventory of these thoughts and note the patterns and repetitions. Where do your thoughts automatically want to go? Does your mind immediately go to the negative possibilities about an event? Do you repeatedly think that people are out to get you? Do you always first think bad things about others? Are you having thoughts about how you appear to others? Worried about what others think about you?

Taking inventory is about stopping when you have a random thought and discerning where it fits. What's your thought pattern? Once you get to this point, you have a greater level of awareness about your mental tendencies. With that awareness, the next time a random thought comes up, you can see it for what it is: a random thought, nothing else, and certainly nothing worth putting much stock into.

Awareness leads to the opportunity to manage. If you're not aware of random thoughts, you cannot manage them. The moment you are aware of them, you can manage and take charge. Once you've taken inventory and notice the patterns to which you're typically subjected, you can begin to create an interrupter to that thought pattern. With that interrupter, ask yourself, "What am I really committed to in the moment? Am I committed to being angry, upset, frustrated, down?" Or "Am I committed to taking action, turning this around, creating a great day for myself?" What is your **commitment**?

This interruption allows you the little bit of space you need to assess the thoughts popping up and to become very mindful of them. It allows you to shift the direction of your thought pattern – from negative to positive… or at least from perceived negativity to "reality." You consciously take control of your thought pattern. Choosing to become responsible for your outcomes puts you in a position of power. You move from being the puppet to the puppeteer.

"You need to learn how to select your thoughts the same way you select your clothes every day. This is a power you can cultivate. If you want to control things in your life so bad, work on the mind. That's the only thing you should be trying to control." ~ Elizabeth Gilbert, *Eat, Pray, Love*

Things to Do Now: Play. Experiment. Sample.

Chapter Three:
Master Your Mind: Who's Pulling Your Strings?

Now that I've introduced the concept of being the puppeteer rather than the puppet (and honestly, no one really wants to be someone's puppet), we're going to dig a bit deeper on the concept of mastering your mind and steps you can take to begin to not only take over the strings but to become skillful at making the puppet move and dance exactly the way you want. A very large part of that is emotional awareness.

When my daughter tells me that her best friend made her mad, I'll stop her and point out that her friend can't do that if she doesn't allow it. Only she can allow her emotions to take over… or not. Her friend can certainly say or do something that triggers a reactive thought in her head that incites an emotion, but my daughter is the only one who can recognize and control the thought that incites the emotion.

Your emotions are the red flags to which you should pay close attention. Emotions are to your mind as pain is to your body. When you feel a physical pain, it's nature's way of telling you something is wrong. It's a red flag, and you need to fix it. You can have any of a myriad of physical pains associated with each of your body's systems – skeletal, digestive, nervous, etc. If a joint or muscle hurts, it's time to stop the activity before you exacerbate an injury. The pain of indigestion causes you to alter your diet. Your body is really good at sending out indicators to make you aware.

So is your mind, but it is up to you to understand and recognize those indicators. Any time you experience mental consternation or a negative emotion, it's a red flag that something needs to be tended to. Negative emotion is to the mind exactly what pain is to the body. A negative emotion – anger, frustration, upset, etc. – is actually a source of pain. It's a clear indicator that something's not right and needs to be fixed.

Your Mind as the Storyteller

Here's a key point to understand in terms of learning to master your mind: Your mind is an excellent storyteller. It has to be. Your mind has to be active. The problem is that the stories your mind comes up with are often unfounded in reality.

As an example, a friend was recently put off because I wasn't speaking much to her one evening at an event. Her mind made up a story about how I was mad at her or dismissing her, so her feelings were hurt. She acted based on those feelings and didn't speak to me for weeks, creating a rift in the friendship. The reality was that I was dealing with a grumpy kid who was taking up a lot of my time and energy… my silence had nothing to do with her or anything she said or did. But her mind made up a completely different story. All of our minds do this. It is how the mind functions when it doesn't have all of the information it needs to create an accurate picture.

There is a huge distinction between events that happen and the subsequent stories the voices in our heads tell us about those events. Our mind makes up a story to try to make sense of and understand the event. The key phrase here is "makes up a story." In turn, the story cultivates the emotional reaction.

The sequence is always: event happens – mind makes up a story about it – emotion ensues. The problem is that middle step. What the voice in your head tells you about the event almost always creates a disconnect between the reality of the event and your emotion about it.

Obviously, we can't control events from happening or not happening. What we can control, and what we need to learn to control to master our minds, is the story that's created about the event. There's a very natural reaction of your brain to try to make sense of your surroundings. That's its job… but your mind often makes errors as a result.

The stories are a direct reaction to the existing context of our minds, existing make up, and previous experiences. Part of this is your own operating system that we'll cover in the next chapter, but a part of it is also driven by your own history. Your perspective is limited by what you've experienced. Our past history dictates our understanding of the events happening around us today.

Most of the time, humans are walking backward into our futures. In other words, we only have what's in the rearview mirror as a reference. Your mind is an index of the experiences and events that help you understand today based on yesterday.

That said, your mind can quickly cultivate a narrative that isn't always accurate! In fact, it's probably more often inaccurate than based in reality, and unless you work at it, your mind will always be limited by your own perspective. Going back to the concept of the puppet and puppeteer, you become the puppet to your past or whomever did something that generated your negative emotion... as in the case of my daughter and her friend. Her friend didn't "make her mad." Instead, my daughter allowed that emotion to take over.

Cutting the Strings

The moment you learn that you completely control the second step in the event/story/emotion sequence – the story your mind creates – you cut the strings and become the puppeteer. You're making up the story anyway, so you can completely control whether that story is negative (driving a negative emotion) or positive, perhaps creating empathy or at least releasing you from anger or frustration.

Let's consider a really common, everyday occurrence: you are cut off in traffic. The typical reaction and story we make up about the event (cutting you off) is that the other driver a rude jerk and they're trying to kill you. What our minds don't typically come up with as the story is that they just got a call that their child was taken to the emergency room and they're on their way to the hospital.

Take a moment to let those two very different scenarios – a.k.a. the story your mind made up – sink in and consider the emotions that you tie to each one. When you let the "jerk trying to kill you" story take over your mind, I'm certain that your teeth clench, your blood pressure goes up, and anger and frustration are the emotions front and center for you. However, if you consider that second scenario, you very likely may feel more empathy and concern... more positive emotions. Notice how each story incites a different emotion.

There are any of a number of other scenarios that can be the *real* cause of someone cutting you off in traffic – late to work because they just learned their spouse is leaving and filing for divorce or they're on their way to visit a parent in hospice. Maybe they simply didn't see you. The reason for the action isn't really the issue. The story your mind makes up about the event is the key. As humans, we're self-referential and the story our minds make up tends to go to the negative... and we become the puppet of a random stranger who cut us off in traffic, and anger and frustration take center stage for the day.

No doubt we've all been treated rudely by a clerk in a store or waitstaff in a restaurant. It's in our nature to immediately take it personally and allow our mind to develop a negative narrative about why the event occurred. They might be having the worst day of their life, perhaps dealing with bad news or even something as simple as they aren't feeling well. There are countless reasons that can cause the event. Human tendency is to only consider the negative.

Of course, the event doesn't have to be driven by a stranger, and often we become puppets to the people in our lives. Let's say your boyfriend/girlfriend is late for your date. Is your immediate imagined story about the reason that they're disrespectful and thoughtless, making you frustrated and furious? Or do you immediately give them the benefit of the doubt for having a good reason, allowing you to be concerned about their welfare?

The key is to stop and consider where your mind goes *first* in making up a story. Once you develop the skill set – really a super power – to **stop** at the moment the narrative is being created in your mind, you can shift your mindset to one that will serve you better. The sequence goes from the typical event/fabricated story/negative emotion to event/STOP and consider the reality around it before allowing your mind to create a narrative/positive emotion and outcome. When you practice that, you develop the super power to be a really good puppeteer.

The Incessant Voice

The narrative that's created about any event that occurs around you is the work of the incessant voice in your head. It's ongoing and is so pervasive. Happening. All. The. Time. Without mastering the mind, few people even recognize that this voice goes on and on and on with little if any real benefit. Most of us don't realize there's a constant narration going on in our heads.

Perhaps I take my dog for a walk, and the narrative may sound like this, "Wow. It's still so humid. When's it going to break? Look at that. I wonder what the neighbor's doing with their house? Why in the world did they pick that color? I haven't seen that neighbor in a while. Maybe I should invite them to dinner. Yeah, a dinner party would be fun. But if I invite them, who else should I invite… or not invite? That guy just drove by way too fast. We should probably have a stop sign at that intersection. Wonder who I contact about that? That reminds me, did I send the tax bill in?"

It's a constant disconnected jumble with one thought colliding with the next one with only a very tangential (if any) connection.

In his book, *The Untethered Soul: The Journey Beyond Yourself*, Michael Singer shares this information:

"If you're smart, you'll take the time to step back, examine the voice, and get to know it better. The problem is, you're too close to be objective. You have to step way back and watch it converse. While you're driving, you hear internal conversations like,

"'Wasn't I supposed to call Fred? I should have. Oh my God. I can't believe I forgot! He's going to be so mad. He many never talk to me again. Maybe I should stop and call him right now. No. I don't want to stop the car right now…'

"Notice that the voice takes both sides of the conversation. It doesn't care which side it takes, just as long as it gets to keep on talking."

We take this narrative as "us," without realizing that we are not our thoughts. We also give credence to the narrative as valid and real. It is not. It's simply entertaining us, and our minds have to be entertained. Without that, we can go a little nutty. The narrative running through our head helps us make sense of the world around us as we encounter it, and it serves as a source of entertainment and engagement. However, be careful! That entertainment can be ill-served. It can be so pervasive and nonstop that it becomes far too automatic. The goal is to control it so that the voice and its narrative is less automatic and more self-directed. ***Once you can direct the voice – master your mind – you can minimize negative mood swings and optimize a more designed outcome for yourself.***

In his book, Michael Singer, really clarifies this concept:

"Thoughts can stop, and they can also get extremely noisy. Sometimes you have many more thoughts than other times. You may even tell someone, 'My mind is driving me crazy. Ever since he said those things to me, I can't even sleep. My mind just won't shut up.' Whose mind? Who is noticing these thoughts? Isn't it you? Don't you hear your thoughts inside? Aren't you aware of their existence? In fact, can't you get rid of them? If you start to have a thought you don't like, can't you try to make it go away?

"People struggle with thoughts all the time. Who is it who's aware of the thoughts? And who is it that struggles with them? There's a subject/object relationship with your thoughts. You're the subject, and the thoughts are just another object you can be aware of. You are not your thoughts. You are simply aware of your thoughts."

Training Your Mind

The best way to train your mind is through meditation. A lot of people get a bit squirrelly about the word "meditation." We can call it stillness or mindfulness; it's the same thing. It's an exercise for your mind.

Once upon a time, the thought of going to the gym to work out your body and get exercise was a ridiculous notion. Back in the day, when the majority were farming the fields and traversing the mountain to grow and hunt for food, that was a natural workout. No need for additional exercise. Without so many of today's conveniences and technology, everything folks did required a great deal of effort and energy. No need for the gym like there is today since so many of us are sedentary for the bulk of the day. Today, it's normal, commonplace, and necessary.

I believe mindfulness practices will become like going to the gym. We'll come to realize there is a need for it. Mindfulness is really the key component you need to train your mind. In fact, most of the top folks in their respective fields have already figured this out. So before you dismiss this or skip ahead, thinking this book has gotten too far afield from the original premise, I assure you, it is all connected.

Don't equate "meditation" with unusual practices that may, or may not, involve yoga and crystals. Very simply, meditation is the practice of controlling your mind over your emotions. If you want to be the puppeteer, you must first control your emotions. As the puppeteer, you take control and will gain the clarity you need to make the best choices for yourself, not only in terms of career choice but throughout your life.

Tim Ferriss, noted podcaster and author of *The 4-Hour Workweek* and many more books, began interviewing 140 different business leaders, asking the same 11 questions, and discovered that the majority had one thing in common. No matter what field they happened to be in, about 90 percent of them practiced meditation – or mindfulness.

As quoted in *Business Insider* for Ferriss's book, *Tribe of Mentors* (compiled from his interviews), he states, "Despite the fact that these are people from tennis to surfing to cryptocurrency to fill-in-the-blank, like any field you can possibly imagine — some type of morning mindfulness or meditation practice would span I'd say 90% of the respondents." A sample of the list of his interviewees includes the founders of Facebook, Twitter, Craigslist, Spotify, and more; Jimmy Fallon; Arianna Huffington; Dara Torres, 12-time Olympic medalist in swimming; Chris Anderson, TED curator; Maria Sharapova, and many more. (See the Resource section for a link to the entire list.)

Ferriss continues, "So meditation, or mindfulness practice, it's really about, to me, decreasing emotional reactivity so you can proactively create your day and create your life; versus, just being a walking reflex that sometimes screws up." Ferriss personally uses a guided meditation from the app Headspace as part of his daily routine. He also attributes his own meditation to his success, including being ranked by *Forbes Magazine* as one of the "Top 25 Small Giants: Best Small Companies in America 2017."

No matter what field you may be interested in – or if, at this point, you are completely unsure – I encourage you to begin the practice of daily mindfulness. Learning to control the voice in your head and your emotions is a key to success. I have plenty of clients who've been in their careers for years or even decades, and when I introduce them to this concept and they begin the practice, they're often sorry they didn't learn this and begin sooner!

Another Tool: Journaling

Meditation is the first tool you can use to train your mind. We've covered a lot about your thoughts; however, your thoughts are rather formless. They come and go, and often do so at random. You can't see them; they're quite intangible. They pop up in an instant and disappear as quickly. This is where journaling becomes a second important tool to use to train your mind.

Journaling helps us take the formlessness of thoughts and put them into a more tangible form. Writing them actually allows you to "see" your thoughts, so you can work more effectively to manipulate them and their patterns. Your thought patterns are as important as the thoughts themselves.

I'm working with a client using the journaling tool, and it is clearly allowing her to uncover her thought patterns. She's journaling and realizing there are certain patterns to her thought process that she was unable to recognize previously.

This tool – journaling – really does help to put structure around those ethereal thoughts that we all have. It provides a way for us to better process the intangible and make it more tangible. When thoughts become more tangible and have more form and structure, suddenly it's easier to modify and manipulate our thoughts… in essence, train our minds. It reveals those areas of thought manipulation that need more work.

When I suggest journaling, people often get stuck. There's a blank sheet or screen staring back at them. What do I do? What do I write about? Do I write about what I had for breakfast? The weather? I ask clients to create inquiries for themselves as a means to get started. For example, "What problem will I solve today?" or "What are three possible solutions to something I'm frustrated about?" And you'll find that there will be plenty of inquiries that arise from this book as you get into the later chapters about the process.

Having used the word "inquiry," I don't want that to be confused with "question to be directly answered." Inquiries are much more open-ended considerations and do not require immediate answers. The idea is to write your thoughts that arise as a result of the inquiry. "What problems will I solve today?" is an inquiry without a consistent answer. It will continually change. Another good inquiry to address each time you journal is "What situations or people do I find most challenging?" Later in the book, I'll ask you to write a letter to yourself from the future. This is also a great journaling starting point as it's a bigger inquiry and gets your stream of thoughts flowing. From one single inquiry will come a number of branched thoughts, ideas, or further inquiries to continue to write about.

When it comes to journaling to train your mind, focus on these bigger sorts of inquiries, not what you had for breakfast. Asking bigger questions also gets you past the blank sheet – the writer's block. When people start with big inquiries in their journaling exercises, the exercise becomes very rewarding. When it's more rewarding you stick with it. The more you stick with it, the better you become at it and at training your mind.

(See the Resource section for a list of questions that will help you journal more effectively.)

Journaling also helps to guide the mind in the direction you want it to go. Again, without training, thoughts are very formless. They're like water and flow wherever. Trying to hold water is impossible... without a container. You cannot mold water without a container and you cannot mold your thinking without using some sort of form like journaling. Journaling allows you to shape and form your thoughts – effectively creating a container or vessel in which to hold them. You can now direct the mind in terms of a) what you want to solve and b) where you want your thoughts to go. This allows you to become a better master of more positive outcomes.

For example, you've just broken up with your romantic partner. You're ruminating about the loss and all of the emotions that go with it. "Why me? What's wrong with me?" And your thoughts go all over the place. Unfortunately, formless thought often turns to the negative and not to problem solving or solutions. Journaling about it allows you to direct those thoughts and your mind more constructively and put tangible form to them. "Okay, there's a reason the relationship didn't work out. What's the reason… or reasons? What is better for me in the future? What do I want that I didn't get from this relationship?" You're now constructively directing your mind on paper. Turning the formlessness of thoughts into a form with recognizable patterns is almost impossible (without a ton of practice) without paper and pen or some form of journaling.

Journaling becomes a tool for managing the mind, but it also becomes a tool to command your mind to be more constructive and to ultimately create better outcomes. It helps to train your mind to be more optimistic because it helps to prevent the perseverance on negative thoughts and replaces them with reconstruction of your ultimate design.

Chapter Four:
Know Yourself: What Is Your Operating System?

In the previous chapter, I opened the door to the concept of managing your mind rather than assuming your mind – your thoughts – are you. Now it's time to walk through that door and explore this further.

Like a computer, I believe every human being has an operating system. The computer doesn't work without an operating system, and like it or not, neither do we. An operating system creates context to organize the immense amount of information taken in. Without an OS, it would be impossible to understand the world around us and our place in it. Our Operating Systems also work hand-in-hand with the voices in our heads. Because of that, it's important to understand your own Operating System, so you can make the best choices for yourself to help you fulfill a life by design. I've coached and counseled plenty of individuals who struggled because they didn't understand how to manage their minds. They also didn't understand that they have what I call a Human Operating System – one that is behind the scenes driving our behavior.

Wouldn't it be crazy if you had the ability to brainwash your own brain... your own mind to have the opportunity to create the career that best suited you and the life of your dreams? This concept – brainwashing your own brain – requires you to complete the exercises of self-awareness to teach you how to manage your own mind. Yes, again I said, "manage your own mind." Think about that one for a moment. Who exactly is doing the thinking if it is about your mind? Is your mind separate from the thinker or a part of it? Perhaps you never thought of your mind as something that could and should be managed – even mastered. Without learning to manage your mind, you are on a path that might not lead you where you want to go.

We all want things in life. I don't necessarily mean material things, but there are ideas or aspirations that we hope to one day realize. Some people dream bigger while others' dreams might be defined as "moderate." Some have grand goals while others are more simplistic. Regardless of the size or complexity of your aspirations, it behooves you to know all you can about how your own mind can help or hinder your goals.

The wild truth about achieving what you want does not necessarily come down to who studies harder, who tries harder, or who works harder. In some cases that may be true, but mostly your success in achievement can be a much straighter line if you understand how your mind operates at its core and how to manage and manipulate it. For most people, achieving success (that is, getting from where they are to where they want to be) is a circuitous route that doubles back on itself at times and takes some erratic turns. If mapped out, it looks far more like a squiggly, meandering line than a straight one. I'm certain you'll agree that a straighter line is the quicker route to success. (Think about those people cited in the previous chapter that were part of Tim Ferriss's work.)

Those who achieve success and have figured out how to travel a straighter line are the ones who've learned how to manage their minds. I have witnessed the impact it has on so many of the lives of people with whom I interact. I, too, have personally experienced the benefits of understanding my particular blind spot about my own Human Operating System and how it literally carved a path for me that had both many benefits but also impeded many areas of my world.

Subjects like these can be tough to comprehend because we are trying to describe or understand something we cannot physically see. It's a lot like your computer or smart phone. Actually, it's like your computer's operating system. You can see your computer and its components, and you can control the components – moving the mouse, keystroking entries, etc. – but what's producing the real results is the operating system. You may think it's a particular software program or app, but without a fully functioning operating system that those programs are written for, it's all pretty useless.

Let me share information from *How Stuff Works*, "How Operating Systems Work" by Curt Franklin and Dave Coustan to paint a clearer picture:

"When you turn on your computer, it's nice to think that you're in control. There's the trusty computer mouse, which you can move anywhere on the screen, summoning up your music library or internet browser at the slightest whim. Although it's easy to feel like a director in front of your desktop or laptop, there's a lot going on inside, and the real man behind the curtain handling the necessary tasks is the operating system.

"Most desktop or laptop PCs come pre-loaded with Microsoft Windows. Macintosh computers come pre-loaded with Mac OS X. Many corporate servers use the Linux or UNIX operating systems. The operating system (OS) is the first thing loaded onto the computer – without the operating system, a computer is useless."

You have an operating system that is also working behind the scenes. And like your computer's operating system, you probably never think about it... until there's a crash, something that derails you on your journey.

One of the other functions of your computer's operating system is to balance resources to keep things moving smoothly. If you're running a software program that demands a lot of memory, your computer's operating system will adjust behind the scenes, so your program runs as it should. The problem with the Human Operating System is that balancing resources is not its proficiency. In fact, the Human Operating System will almost always direct resources to accomplish one task: cover up insecurity.

Human Operating Systems

While we all have a Human Operating System (HOS), there are a number of different ones. In fact, I've defined at least ten different Operating Systems over the years in my work with clients, and I've covered these in-depth in my book, *The Hijacker, Overcome Self-Sabotaging Behavior*. Despite their differences in how they manifest in the traits and patterns that people exhibit and how they might be self-sabotaging their own efforts to achieve the life they want, every one of these operating systems works to accomplish one thing: Human Operating Systems work to cover up insecurity.

We all have insecurities, and those insecurities may plague students and young adults to an even greater degree. You may look at adults you know or even someone famous that you believe is completely without insecurity because of the way they act, what they say, and how they handle themselves. Based on their actions, you find it difficult, if not impossible, to believe that they could have any insecurities at all.

And that's exactly the point! It is their Human Operating System working full steam ahead to hide their greatest insecurity.

Once you understand the various operating systems, you'll be able to identify the one you have, and that is the first step in learning to manage it… the first step toward Conscious Discernment. Conscious Discernment is having the ability to be fully aware of your choices and make the proper choice that is in alignment with your bigger commitments. When you are unaware of your unconscious drivers, when you have too many blind spots, when you're unclear about your HOS, you don't have the ability to practice Conscious Discernment. You may think you have a clear design on what you want out of your life, including your career aspirations, but I submit that that design is still a result of your unconscious driver – what I call the hijacker of your life. Unless you've had your Human Operating System identified and brought into the forefront of your consciousness, it's still running your life in the background… and will continue to do so until you take control by managing your mind.

While I've likened your Human Operating System to that of a computer, there is a major and fundamental difference between the two. The computer is entirely and completely objective. It carries out commands without feeling a need to survive. It is after all, mathematically based and very logical.

On the other hand, your brain, the center of your own operating system, is anything but. Sure, you can be logical at times, but in general, humans are emotional, reactive beings. It's the way we're wired. You see, most of us believe we think things through; however, the truth is that most of us are walking zombies, reacting to the world around us through our various filters.

Now, here's the weird thing: Your Operating System – that was created by some event when you were very young – also has a strong survival mechanism. Believe it or not, your Operating System can become threatened when challenged. If it feels threatened, it will fight for its own survival. This is the root of why we sabotage ourselves. It will fight to keep the status quo. Not so with a computer. It doesn't perceive threat and it has no survival instinct. It chugs along making the calculations it was designed to make. Humans simply don't work that way. For every Operating System, when the human behind it becomes aware of how to manage it and begins to do so, the Human Operating System's survival mechanism kicks in and tries to fight for its own survival. It will attempt to affirm the insecurity behind the HOS. Bear in mind that your HOS is a significant part of your identity. When your Operating System is challenged, it "fights" back to help maintain your known identity. This is critical to understand.

Your mind will find evidence for whatever it believes to be true. It will make all else an exception. Your mind will exaggerate that which supports your Operating System and dismiss even the hardest, truest facts that don't support it.

There is no objectivity. It's all part of its survival mechanism. It's all part of maintaining your current identity that ultimately includes perceived limits of success in academics, relationships, and other accomplishments.

Operating System Overviews

Let me give you a broad overview of the various Human Operating Systems, so you begin to see where yours is and may also recognize the Operating Systems of others in your life as well.

Unlovable:

You might never make the connection between those with an Unlovable Operating System and their actions. Unlovable HOS people are very nurturing and caring. They prefer a few very deep relationships as opposed to several more "general" friendships. I see a lot of nurses, grade school teachers, and charitable volunteers who operate under the Unlovable HOS.

Powerless:

Many presidents and those in executive positions are going through life with Powerless Operating Systems. Politicians striving to seek higher and higher positions? Place your bet on a Powerless HOS. But it isn't just success in business or politics. These people can be very active in physical conditioning, martial arts, or anything else that contributes to being perceived as and feeling powerful.

Incompetent:

Those with an Incompetent HOS seem to be good (if not great!) at whatever they do. Think about extraordinary athletes, like LeBron James, just to name one who exceeded and worked to reach the pinnacle of his sport. These people are usually at the top of their game – whatever their game may be: head trainer, captain of the team, head of their class, etc.

Ugly:

I doubt you would have figured Marilyn Monroe as having an Ugly HOS, but I would place her in this category. Ugly people don't like to leave the house without being well manicured, made up, not a hair out of place, and perfectly coordinated. You can even spot them at the gym because their workout attire resembles that of a runway model.

Unlikeable:

If you want to better understand who is operating under an Unlikeable HOS, peruse Facebook or Instagram and see who has the most friends/followers (or most connections on LinkedIn or most followers on Twitter). Popularity comes naturally to those with this operating system. It is a by-product of their "connecting" skills. People just gravitate toward those with this HOS. An Unlikeable HOS is the perfect make up for a successful salesperson.

Weak:

The World's Strongest Man competition is filled with those operating under the Weak HOS, and it's not limited to the male gender. Muscles, muscles, and more muscles. They live at the gym and tout health food and other muscle-building solutions. Strength and health are paramount.

Dumb:

As you're reading through these generalized descriptions, you're quickly making the connection between the HOS classification and the opposite traits. The Dumb HOS is no exception. Dumb types often have many letters or acronyms (i.e., degrees and certifications) after their names. They like to use very big words that send the rest of us to the dictionary. When you read a book authored by someone with a Dumb HOS, you will find yourself spending as much time in the dictionary as in their book. Grade point average? 4.5, because 4.0 isn't good enough.

Outcast:

Those with an Outcast HOS are always in the mix. Their fear of missing out on... well, anything is what drives them. They are constantly on the go with a social schedule chock full of parties and gatherings. Going out is their life. Being unique is a vital element to this type. It is better to stand out than to fade into the crowd.

Failure:

Success after success defines those with the Failure HOS. People like J.D. Rockefeller, who are amazing at what they can create in terms of developing and managing businesses and their success, operate with a Failure HOS. Often Failures actually have one successful business after another.

Bad:

The person with the Bad HOS is a pleaser, and for them, every last detail has to be perfect and every rule followed to the Nth degree. There's a lot of stress for those with this HOS because perfection, though aspired by this type, is almost always impossible to achieve.

HOS Types at a Glance

Area of Dominance	HOS Type	Traits
Social Dominant	Unlikeable	Lots of friends (virtual and real world) Active social calendar Great conversationalist / "life of the party" Proverbial salesperson
	Unlovable	Caring/nurturing Self-sacrificing Generous Fewer but deeper friendships
	Bad	Rule follower "Put together" Pleaser Nice
	Outcast	Active social life Unique, stand-out traits Values individuality More unconventional

Success Dominant	Failure	Monetarily driven Desires the finer things Fancy cars, homes, watches, etc. Winning is a priority
	Powerless	High position of power Natural leader Not subservient Also likes winning
	Incompetent	Ability driven Wide range of abilities Finish on top Fiscally smart – researches all purchases
Appearance Dominant	Ugly	Perfectly "put together" Detail person Coordinator Coiffed Perfect party planner
	Weak	Strong All about physicality Fitness is a priority Uses nutritional supplements "Gym rat"

Know Yourself: What Is Your Operating System?

Intelligence Dominant	Dumb	Fact driven A "go-to" source for information Research-oriented Walking dictionary

With this generalized overview, you may be able to pick out your own HOS. Before you are too quick to think about many of the negative or less attractive traits that were mentioned and wave them all off, believing that none of those applies to you (or that you have some of every single one, so no one HOS truly defines you), let me take a minute to remind you of what a Human Operating System really is.

Like computers, we *all* have operating systems working behind the scenes. Without the operating system in a computer, all of the helpful, supportive, and cool apps and software that are available are entirely useless. Also like a computer, sometimes the Human Operating System needs a tune up or a full reboot. If you are anything like me, I don't consider rebooting my computer or smartphone until it starts to get quirky or not operate effectively and ignore the fact that rebooting on a regular basis is healthy for the effective operation of my devices. Cleaning up and refreshing the system can help prevent the dreaded system crash.

Your Personality and Design

In addition to your own particular HOS, there are personality types that overlay with it. They may align as you'd think they would. For example, someone with an Unlikeable HOS is typically outgoing, but that is not necessarily a tried-and-true connection.

At this point in your life, you probably have a pretty good handle on your own personality: introvert vs. extrovert; talkative vs. quiet; optimistic vs. pessimistic; patient vs. impatient; fearless vs. conservative, etc. If you aren't certain, you can certainly ask your family and friends how they see you. Knowing your personality type is another puzzle piece that goes into creating and designing the right career choice for yourself. ***Your personality is an important ingredient.***

Additionally, you have environments and activities that you enjoy and prefer. Although some may seem preferable – and cooler on social media, like rock climbing over reading – you do yourself a huge disservice by not being honest about what you really like. If you like reading, so be it, and if that's the case, I assure you, it is not "less cool" than rock climbing.

Take into consideration your preferred focus: clearly defined tasks that may be repetitive or more varied and perhaps more challenging; working alone toward a goal or the need to collaborate and be part of a team. Like personality, there is no right or wrong. The best ingredient is the one that works for you. You simply have to take time to define it.

Do you like to travel and have wanderlust that makes you want to see and experience new places? Or are you more of a homebody, with roots that go pretty deep? Again, neither is right nor wrong. Honestly admitting you're more comfortable as a homebody does not mean you'll never travel or see the world. Likewise, the person who wants to leave home and live in different areas with different cultures is not abandoning family and heritage.

Consider your hobbies also. They are also indicators of your personality. The student who lists reading as a hobby might be the quiet type – although that's also a stereotype, so never assume that to be the case. The same is true of the adventurer who is the talkative extrovert. Whatever your hobbies and interests, they are solid indicators of your likes as well as your skills. Enjoy coaching little league? You might excel at leadership. Enjoy spending time alone working with technology? You might be a good fit for IT, but a social job may not be up your alley. Enjoy puzzles? Problem solving is likely a great fit.

Keep in mind that your personal life (including hobbies and interests) and your career are not separate entities. They are inseparable. Embracing this leads to career satisfaction; ignoring it leads in the other direction.

Finally, consider your future design. Where do you want to live? Maybe you had a really positive vacation experience in a destination that has stuck with you, and you always figured you'd return there to live. Or you have experience with a particular area based on visiting family members and enjoy the location. Perhaps you aren't drawn to a particular city or locale but know the type of geography and weather you like – sunny and warm or plenty of snow.

What have been your expectations about your own family life desires? Kids? No kids? Maybe start a family later? How much mobility do you envision for yourself? Can you foresee time constraints?

Granted, this may all be very uncertain at this point in your life and it may change, but now is the time to a least consider what you want your life to look like. And we're going to start exploring that more fully in the next chapter.

Chapter Five:
The Process: Identifying Your Ingredients

Hopefully, you did not simply jump ahead to this chapter and have truly considered and absorbed the information from the previous chapters. Understanding how your mind works and actually training your own mind as well as considering that you have an internal operating system are critical components to really designing a career choice that indeed works for you. Designing your career is integral to designing your entire life, one that brings you happiness and fulfillment. In essence, everything we've covered to this point is actually part of "the process," but now we'll start to get down to the nuts and bolts and even put pen to paper.

But before we do that, I want to take another moment to talk a bit more about mindset, specifically a fixed vs. a growth mindset. With a fixed mindset, you believe that your basic abilities, intelligence, and talents are fixed... carved in stone and that's that. In a growth mindset, you believe that your abilities and intelligence can be developed and furthered with effort, learning, and persistence. Obviously, a growth mindset is required to break outside of where you are at this point. The challenge is always to foster a growth mindset.

One path to developing your growth mindset is to decide that it's time to stop thinking what everyone else is thinking and shut down any herd mentality you may have. This can be particularly difficult for teens who have an almost innate need to fit in with their peers and conform. However, the herd reflects a fixed mindset and following the herd is essentially picking from the short menu – the kids' menu. There's no real thought or effort needed. The herd all moves in the same direction, so you don't need to stop and think about navigation or the best way to get there. You just go with the flow. When you're following the herd, the path is beaten down and well-worn, so traveling it is easier… no need to cut a new trail and no bushwhacking required. That path may be easy, but it's also pretty boring and may not take you anywhere near where *you* really want to go.

This is why I've spent so much time to this point on the need to master your mind. When you train your mind to think creatively, you pick and pull from different inputs to allow you to think outside the box. It's the very nature of creativity. We may all be exposed to the same inputs, but it's how we arrange them that makes a difference. For example, there are only so many musical notes – a dozen, in fact. We all have access to the same dozen notes when composing, but how we put them together creates the difference between "Twinkle, Twinkle Little Star" that uses only about half of them and Beethoven's Symphony No. 9.

Every time we can pick and choose and rearrange various inputs, we create something new – a new idea, product, design, artwork, story, composition, etc. When we're creative, we are breaking away from herd mentality and developing a growth mindset. Yes, it takes effort and thought and even hard work, but it is the only way to design the career and life of your choice. And it's not typically what you've been exposed to up to this point in your life.

Consider public education. It is designed to teach the masses and is the proverbially scaled business. By having a scaled business and, for example, a teaching approach with set worksheets – identical for every child – it eliminates creativity. With this approach, we're programming students rather than facilitating their own thinking processes. This is nothing new, and as I'm authoring this, we are in the middle of the coronavirus pandemic. With schools closed, I'm now homeschooling my first grade daughter. Since we're working one-on-one, I can get really creative with the sources of inputs to help her understand the concepts and then arrange and rearrange the inputs for more creativity on her part... rather than simply going through lessons worksheet by worksheet. The upside to the worksheet-by-worksheet approach (whether in the classroom or homeschooling) is that it's very streamlined and consistent. It can be delivered to thousands of kids. The downside is that it does not facilitate creative thinking that ultimately leads to innovation. Mass education also means a lot of rules imposed by administration to minimize "disruption" to other students.

Being a sheep does not allow for the creativity needed to introduce and mix new ingredients to add a more robust flavor to your recipe. You may turn out a solid meal, but you may get bored of it quickly. Working off the same worksheets as everyone else limits your knowledge and context to that of everyone else. Break the walls of conformity and discover a new, richer blend of flavors.

So how does this relate to the process of career choice? Don't be a sheep, always going where the herd goes. Instead challenge the status quo. Consistently ask why. Yes, there may be a good reason for doing something a particular way; however, "because we've always done it that way" is a really bad answer. In fact, it's the worst answer. Also, be tuned into every experience, even the negative ones. Learning what you don't want is as important as learning what you do want.

Creativity and Critical Thinking

When I discovered in my master's program that the path I was on wasn't going to be one I wanted to continue traveling, I had to go back and check the "ingredients" I had at hand. With cooking, there is a level of creativity. You get familiar with the basic ingredients and then decide to add a dash of this, a pinch of that. Give it a taste and decide it needs a bit more of another flavor. This is the piece I believe is sorely missing when it comes to career choice. We don't really facilitate the creative part of the process, so it's impossible to develop an individualized career. You need to continue to add input on your own so that you can become more creative with a greater variety of ingredients. If you only have chicken and a heat source (bake, broil, or poach), it makes a pretty bland meal. When you add any number of great spices and sauces, you can cook up something far more delicious.

The only way to be creative is to add new sources of input – new ingredients. What are those? In essence, they are every experience you've ever had. This is exactly why I encourage internships and ask you to focus on all of the things you've done (both work and recreation) and then evaluate those experiences as the "ingredients" you tested. This is why one of the first things we covered in the book was the importance of playing, experimenting, and sampling.

Critical thinking also plays a major role in your ability to discern your ingredients. Unfortunately, critical thinking is often not reinforced in school. So how can you hone your own critical thinking skills? You can do that through new inputs – things like puzzles, creative exercises, new inquiries, and brainstorming… anything that gets your mind thinking beyond the box and beyond your current perspectives.

This takes you from a sealed or locked way of learning in which you learn what everybody else learns (the worksheet approach), so you move from the core knowledge (the chicken) to attaining new inputs (spices and sauces). This is exactly what the innovators of the world do. Consider the founders of Uber. Its development went through various iterations, but it was created through inquiry: How do we combine the need for taxi service and unused or idle vehicles sitting in someone's driveway or garage? The likes of Thomas Edison, Benjamin Franklin, Elon Musk, Steve Jobs, Nikola Tesla, Bill Gates – any great inventor or innovator – all created by inquiry. What if….? Keep asking questions.

Know Your Ingredients and Take Inventory

Your creativity and critical thinking ability are two of the main ingredients. School provides you with the basic recipe. Perhaps when cooking, a recipe calls for a teaspoon of salt. You may choose to stick with that or you may choose to get more creative, using more or less salt or substituting it with garlic salt or truffle salt seasoning instead. It's really up to you to get creative with the ingredients – the knowledge

The Process: Identifying Your Ingredients

and experience – you have. Lacking this creativity is where people get stuck... and revert back to the kids' menu in their career choices. This can lead to a life of bland choices that don't quite satisfy your palate.

In choosing a career, first understand that your education provides you with the recipe and the fundamentals of cooking. You know the subjects at which you excel and enjoy. Now it's time to take inventory of your "cabinets or pantry" to determine what you have on hand in order to spice it up. Plus, you'll have to figure out how to creatively combine ingredients to come up with something really great – something that suits you and adds flavor to your life.

In addition to your awareness about which subjects you enjoy in school, you probably have previous work experience (i.e., part-time or volunteering) that will play a part in your decision. In the section below, list all of these positions along with a word or two about what you specifically liked and disliked about each.

Position	Likes:	Dislikes:

In creating a sauce for basic chicken, most recipes start with flour or corn starch. This represents what you enjoy – hobbies and interests. We often separate this from career; however, hobbies draw a direct link to where we derive enjoyment and how we like to spend time. Too often, the thought is that our career is something we go and do and it's serious and it's work while hobbies are something we do in our free time after work. That thinking is a mistake. Consider instead the advice "pick something you love and you'll never *work* a day in your life." Seriously consider your hobbies in your career choice process. With that said, it can be challenging to distinguish between hobbies and long-term career satisfaction, but hobbies provide insight into the ingredients we need in our career recipe.

Take a moment to list your hobbies and interests and try to keep them in order of importance, starting with what you enjoy most and participate in most often:

1)

2)

3)

4)

5)

6)

Review your list and determine if there is any theme to the items on it. There is almost always a pattern or cadence to the things we enjoy. Take my list for example: gardening,

The Process: Identifying Your Ingredients

psychology, business, home renovation, paddle boarding, boating, walking, cycling….

I am able to find a couple of patterns – outdoor activity, water, strategy, and transformation. You will soon recognize that some things were meant to remain a recreational interest and others that are career worthy. It took me several years to recognize that there was a similar satisfaction I got from transforming things. I enjoy transforming my houses, minds, and businesses.

I've seen lists where being visually creative was a critical element that emerged as a common thread. Others I've seen: animals, athletics, social contribution and so on. The themes are there; it is up to you to uncover them.

Another basic ingredient consists of your core needs. What have you discovered about yourself and your needs through the experiences and jobs you've already had? Perhaps it's having a consistent routine. I had one client who had an opportunity to work for a great company, but it involved shift work. He knew he needed a consistent routine from week to week, so that was out of consideration for him. Another core need may be work/life balance. You need to determine this for yourself. For some, they want to be able to shut down and leave "work" at the office at the end of the day, so an 8:00 to 5:00 job in a specific place works well for them. For others, that concept is far too constricting. They have a core need for greater flexibility. They have a need to come and go throughout the day and aren't bothered when work and non-work time are more intertwined. Also, consider the time of day when you are at your best. Some are early birds who don't work well and don't feel smart at night; some are night owls who don't really hit all cylinders until later in the day.

Really define your needs. Yes, by doing so, as my client learned by passing on the opportunity that required shift work, you will lock out and eliminate certain things that may be perfectly fine… for someone else. You must define this for yourself. It's foundational. The more you define, the simpler the decision can be.

Consider your own core needs (e.g., night owl vs. morning lark, structured day vs. flexibility/changeability, etc.):

_____
_____
_____
_____
_____

One other basic ingredient needed to determine how to best tweak your recipe is to ask what you absolutely loathe. We've covered your hobbies and interests, so uncovering what you really dislike is actually very, very helpful. For some, it's the idea of sales. Anything related to selling is a complete turn off. For others working in isolation is loathsome. Perhaps feeling like the low man on the totem ball is a non-starter while others hate the idea of lacking guidance. In my case, I would loathe constant travel for my career, but I know there are others who would hate to sit at a desk in an office every day.

The Process: Identifying Your Ingredients

There is no right or wrong, so be very honest as you note what you really hate (e.g., working with blood, not being able to interact with people, being location dependent, working in the _____ field, etc.):

_____
_____
_____
_____
_____
_____

With those basics in place, let's start to add some spices to our ingredient list. To do so, we'll start with character traits. These represent the way we behave on a consistent basis. Your HOS will come into play here as well. Consider this partial list and determine which apply to you and define you:

Inventive	Sensitive
Outgoing	Confident
Efficient	Compassionate
Curious	Courageous
Cautious	Adventurous
Organized	Unselfish
Easy going	Loyal
Exacting	Faithful
Energetic	Kind
Reserved	Ambitious
Friendly	Optimistic
Solitary	Resourceful

Decisive   Quiet
Bold   Organized

Add anything you feel is a character trait not included on the list above:
_____
_____

While we covered your hobbies as a basic ingredient, one of the spices is to know what intrigues you. What is it that you never tire learning about? For me, the mind and the brain and how they work are incredibly intriguing. I am always on the lookout for more information on these topics. My interest about the mind is insatiable. For some people, it may be language and words – the way they go together to express a concept or create a poem. It may be animal behavior and natural sciences. Many are intrigued by the way things work – how they're put together and why they operate the way they do. Technology is very intriguing to some while others don't really care how it works as long as they can use the app.

What intrigues you?_____
_____
_____

Your desired lifestyle is another important spice to consider. This works in conjunction with your needs, but it is a bit more nuanced; it reflects more of your choice than a need. I want you to understand that all of this represents "and" type of thinking. You can have this ***and*** that. You are not limited to this *or* that. Don't lock out the possibilities by thinking "*or*" is your only choice.

When my husband and I were considering our desired lifestyle when creating our business, we wanted to be free of the constraints of location. Location was a lifestyle choice for us. We enjoy owning businesses and had the opportunity to buy an iconic bakery up north. This bakery had been in business for over 100 years. It was coveted by people everywhere – and it was up for sale. While owning the business would have been great, it also meant we would be glued to that locale year-round... and we had no desire to spend winters in Michigan.

Everyone has some defining aspect of their envisioned lifestyle. One client had a visceral reaction against leaving Manhattan. There were several great opportunities in his area of interest, but they were outside of New York City. The location actually defined him. As a result, he accepted that this limited his ingredients and the ability to alter the recipe. He knew he was passing up some great opportunities; however, he also knew the lifestyle he wanted and it revolved around being in the Big Apple.

For some, the calling may be the mountains or the water. The career choice may not necessarily rely on being in those places, but it is where they are most at home and it is part of their entire life experience. Respect this important ingredient because when people ignore a core aspect that defines them, ultimately consternation arises because a need is unfulfilled.

Delineate your ideal lifestyle (e.g., family structure, location, activities you enjoy [perhaps location-based; e.g., boating, hiking, skiing, golfing, etc.]):

_____
_____
_____
_____
_____
_____
_____

Another spice to consider is your work environment, and this is typically defined by the work experiences you've already had, either good or bad. One client wanted to investigate business coaching; however, when she thought about working virtually, she knew it wasn't for her. She had to be in the mix, face-to-face, and not simply on the phone all the time. It was a critical factor that we needed to consider. But… that didn't mean there wasn't an alternative. Remember "and" thinking; it doesn't have to be either/or. There are plenty of opportunities that can be molded to include this *and* that. For example, sports teams now rely on and employ mindset coaches for players, and there is a similar need in the corporate world as well. So, she could continue to pursue the idea of coaching, just not as a virtual coach. On the other hand, I'm perfectly happy and prefer to work virtually from my home office, not having to leave the house.

Consider you the ideal work environment in which you see yourself:

_____
_____
_____

The Process: Identifying Your Ingredients

Before we go further, I want you to take a moment, having read this far, to create a list of **all** the vocations that you've considered and determine why they crossed your mind as a potential choice or why you might be crossing them off now. (Use another sheet of paper if you need more space.) Also indicate if you'll keep any of your listed vocations for consideration or remove from your list. Keep in mind that this is a work in progress. Your choices right now might look like "the kids' menu"; however, as we continue to go through the book, you will continue to refine your choice – your ingredients and recipe – to become some much more delectable.

Vocation	Why?	Why Not?	Keep?(Y/N)

The Staircase Concept

As you are considering your basic ingredients and the spices that will jazz things up and move you beyond the kids' menu, I want to take a moment to explain what I call the "staircase" concept. No matter how hard you work to determine the best path forward for yourself, as you are choosing a major or graduating from college, your plan of study or career choice will likely evolve in the future. And having read this far, your reaction to that suggestion may be: "Whhaaattt?"

Yes, things change and things will always evolve. But there is a very misguided sense that when things do change, you have to start all over. Wrong.

As long as you choose the right staircase – and "staircase" is a metaphor for your fundamental career choice or course of study – in the first place (which is exactly what this book is designed to help you do), you'll be okay.

You'll find that there is an ongoing progression or evolution from the general to something more specific. When you apply what you've learned in this book and complete the exercises I suggest, you'll find yourself at the foot of the correct staircase, so you'll simply have to start climbing or climb a few more steps as things evolve to reach the right destination – it's a progression, one step at a time. For those who don't do the things I'm suggesting in this book and apply what they've learned, they very well may find themselves on the wrong staircase, in which case, they *will* have to climb back down, find a new staircase, and start over.

I'll use my brother as a great example of the staircase concept. He was a mechanic and, as a kid, he tinkered on cars and took things apart and put them back together. He loved to fix things – it was always a common thread for him. At age 16, being a car mechanic was the career he loved. There was a constant thread of evidence through his experiences. As a teenager, he delivered car parts for an automotive store. He "sup'd-up" every vehicle he owned (even those he didn't own – like mine). He spent time in the Navy where is chose to work on aircraft (yes, the Navy has aircraft). After the military, he took a civilian job working for Northwest Airlines fixing aircraft. However, by the time he was 40, he had other ideas and did not want to be a mechanic for the rest of his life. That said, mechanics was still the right staircase for him. His progression was from car mechanic to airline mechanic to now building plane engines at GE He could have dismissed everything once fixing cars became boring for him, but mechanics always remained the correct staircase. He simply had to continue to progress to new steps, and as he did so, his career evolved, but he was never faced with "starting over."

Envision moving up a staircase and being at the top of where you want to be. The goal of this book and the exercises I want you to complete is to lead you to the right staircase – the one *you* should begin to climb either through your choice of college major or actual career.

Visit a Magazine Rack

I've already talked about diving into the topics or arenas that you can't get enough of. In my case, I've always been intrigued by the mind and human behavior and can't

Find Your Flavor

get enough of the topic. Of course, I have interests in many other topics as well. I'm sure the same is true for you, so now it's time to visit a magazine rack to help you really determine the right staircase for yourself. And yes, I mean a physical magazine rack at your local bookstore or somewhere similar.

Pull out all of the magazines that are of interest – all of them, regardless how diverse the topics may be. And yes, it's okay to make judgments based on their covers. Now sit down with that stack of magazines and notice those that you want to read cover-to-cover… those in which every single article is of interest to you and you won't put it down until you've read them all. Set those aside. By doing this, you'll narrow a pile of perhaps as many as ten or 20 down to two or three. It will be two or three that you really want to subscribe to and always read front-to-back when every single issue arrives. These selections have uncovered a sense of your lasting intrigue, and lasting intrigue equals your staircase.

In my brother's case, to this day, he still reads about and researches vehicles and enjoys it. When I need to shop for a car, I know he is my best resource and one who's rock solid. In my own case, when I do the magazine rack exercise, I would select remodeling magazines (e.g., *Homes and Gardens, House Beautiful,* etc.) and any that focus on renovations. I would also pick up *Entrepreneur* and *Psychology Today*. I really enjoy renovating and decorating and enjoy paging through those magazines, but I don't read them cover-to-cover. I might read an article that is specific to a project that I'm undertaking but never take the time to read the entire magazine. However, when I pick up *Psychology Today* and *Entrepreneur*, I read every issue in their entirety... every single month. It is the difference between my interests and my intrigue.

I find there is a similar uncovering of the discernment between interest and intrigue when it comes to sports. A lot of the students I coach tell me they love sports. But it becomes readily apparent when we go through the magazine exercise that while they might enjoy spectating a particular sport, they are not interested in a deep study of it. They might read an article or two about a favorite player or watch a game, but they're not reading everything month after month. The student who's reading an article or two is interested; the one who is reading everything and studying the strategy of the game at a deep level is intrigued.

Even at age seven, we're seeing a pattern of intrigue in my daughter. She doesn't pick up and read a lot of different books cover-to-cover... except when it comes to science. Then she is fully engaged, watching video after video on an array of science topics and reading about the human body. She can't get enough; she's clearly intrigued. A lot of people get caught up in chasing interests but can become bored with them. On the other hand and the important differentiator: ***intrigue lasts forever***.

Before going further, it's to your benefit to complete this exercise now.

Find Your Flavor

List the magazines that first attracted you and that you consider reading:

From above, now list the magazines to which you'd pay to subscribe and wouldn't feel like you'd be wasting your money:

From above, next list the magazines you'd read cover-to-cover:

With the pared down list of those magazines you'd read cover-to-cover, you are zeroing in on your main ingredient. It is an indicator of what truly intrigues you.

Fusion Cuisine

Fusion cuisine deliberately combines elements of various culinary traditions that originate from different cultures or parts of the world. Think: taco pizza, pastrami egg rolls, spaghetti tacos, kimchi quesadilla. Foods that you might never have thought of combining that create a very memorable dish. You get the picture.

Keep the fusion concept in mind if you happen to uncover two areas of intrigue for yourself. In my own example, my intrigues are business and psychology. I didn't have to choose between one or the other and ultimately created a career that combined the two – a fusion.

Look for crossovers if you happen to have two areas that are truly intriguing to you. Although they may seem disparate (like Asian and Mexican dishes), you can combine them to create something quite different and quite delicious – far, far from the kids' menu. It's where you begin to fine-tune and create a fusion in your own recipe. Remember: Never limit yourself to "either/or" thinking. Use "and" thinking instead.

So many people get stuck making the distinction between interest and intrigue. Typically, the answer lies in past experiences, which is why I always ask my clients to discuss not just previous work experiences but ***all*** experiences they've had. However, at this point in your life, it is critical to gain as many different experiences as you can. Experiences are a key component to uncovering the elements you're looking for in a career, including working style and environment.

Experiences layer on top of the subject matter, like spices layering on the main ingredient. Your main ingredient is the thing you need to study deeply to become a true professional. Experience helps to provide insight, but the problem is that we can't test out everything to really get a handle on intrigue. That's why the magazine rack exercise helps – it creates a needed shortcut.

You will find that the magazine exercise suddenly helps you gain insight into why you've done certain things or have been attracted to certain things throughout your life. This exercise alone begins to open the cabinet of your ingredients to see what you've done to date and what you need to do more of – whether that becomes a field of study, your major, or the industry in which you should be pursuing an internship. These things then point you in the direction of your staircase and help you to clearly differentiate between interest and intrigue. For me, I was interested in law, but a summer internship in a law office quickly clarified that while it was an interest, it was definitely not intriguing enough for me to continue pursuing it.

Intrigue = Main Ingredient

Once you determine your area(s) of intrigue, you're honing your main ingredient. You're picking between chicken, steak, seafood, or vegan. Now it's time to introduce yourself to your chosen arena, and that can be done through an internship, shadowing someone you know in the profession, part-time job, volunteering, etc.

Once you solidify your main ingredient (or your staircase to return to that analogy), it's time to start choosing your spices that are going to create the perfect recipe for you. While plenty of people may have the same main ingredient, there are countless spices that can combine to create very different dishes. When we think about the kids' menu for example, chicken is always in the form of chicken fingers or nuggets. That's not to say chicken is a boring main ingredient. It's not. It's simply time to spice things up. Depending on the spices you choose, you can create two wildly different tasting dishes from the same main ingredient. Someone may love chicken Parmesan while someone else prefers chicken Piccata – same main ingredient but very different end results in terms of taste... all driven by the spices.

You may choose a certain recipe today (e.g., Parmesan) and will find that your tastes change and evolve, and in the future, you may gravitate toward something else (e.g., Piccata). That evolution is never a problem as long as you have the correct main ingredient. However, for many people, as they begin to evolve – if something doesn't work out as expected or they hit a roadblock – they begin to question their main ingredient or staircase. In reality, they don't need to change the main ingredient, they simply need to alter the spices. Too many people are conditioned to believe that if a particular opportunity doesn't work out, they have to start over completely rather than refine what they've already done. The idea of simply refining is a huge relief, especially for a lot of my adult clients. They were working with the right main ingredient all along. It provides them with the confidence they need to alter their own recipe and move forward again, rather than becoming paralyzed and worried they've wasted their time.

For example, someone may have pursued medicine and becoming a doctor was always their focus – one that admittedly takes a lot of time and commitment. Perhaps they also loved kids, so they narrowed their focus to pediatrics. They get through the internships and residencies, pass the board, and hang out their shingle… only to realize that practicing pediatric medicine isn't what they thought it would be and they find no passion in it. Should they give up their license to practice medicine and start over? No. They simply need to shift a bit and look for other spices. Maybe it's the hours they have to keep or maybe they realize that they don't love kids as much as they thought they did. Or maybe it is pediatrics but in a different format, like research.

Your Main Ingredient

It's time to do your homework and start listing some of the main ingredients that would be the right one for you on which to build out your recipe – your career.

Take the time to write them down and determine what you can do to test them – to make sure they're not only palatable to you but that they truly represent the right staircase for you. Again, as you are creating your list, keep in mind whether it's something that interests or intrigues you.

Next to each one, figure out how you can play with it. Are there part-time jobs, internships, courses and classes, shadowing or volunteer opportunities, etc. that will give you a realistic taste? What magazines from the earlier exercise align with each? Read those magazines or follow blogs or podcasts that focus on each. Are you hanging on every word or getting bored halfway through?

Start taking classes or considering the class structure of your desired field. The required courses for pursuing a degree represent your main ingredient. Then consider the electives that you can pair with it the way you would pair spices with chicken, beef, seafood, or tofu.

Someone who is pursuing a degree in business might opt for an elective that focuses on debate or public speaking if they are thinking of a career as a business coach or corporate trainer. This can add a layer to refine the career choice. It can also steer you away from a spice that is a mismatch. If you take a course in public speaking and dread every moment of it, sweating to get through the class, it doesn't mean business is the wrong choice. It simply means that having a more public persona might not be right for you… or it is something to which you haven't evolved yet.

Now, using your main ingredients uncovered in the previous exercises, list ten possible "jobs," businesses, or vocations that might fall under each on. Under each of those, jot a note about how you might get a taste of it (e.g., part-time job, internship, classes, volunteer or shadowing opportunities):

Main Ingredient: _____

1) _____

How to sample:

_____
_____

2) _____

How to sample:

_____
_____

3) _____

How to sample:

_____
_____

4) _____

How to sample:

_____
_____

5) _____

How to sample:

_____
_____

6) _____

How to sample:

_____
_____

7) _____

How to sample:

_____
_____

8) _____

How to sample:

_____
_____

9) _____

How to sample:

_____
_____

10) _____

The Process: Identifying Your Ingredients

How to sample:

_____
_____

Main Ingredient: _____

   1) _____

     How to sample:

_____
_____

   2) _____

     How to sample:

_____
_____

   3) _____

     How to sample:

_____
_____

   4) _____

     How to sample:

_____
_____

   5) _____

     How to sample:

_____
_____

   6) _____

     How to sample:

_____
_____

7) _____

How to sample:
_____
_____

8) _____

How to sample:
_____
_____

9) _____

How to sample:
_____
_____

10) _____

How to sample:
_____
_____

Main Ingredient: _____

1) _____

How to sample:
_____
_____

2) _____

How to sample:
_____
_____

3) _____

The Process: Identifying Your Ingredients

How to sample:

_____
_____

4) _____

How to sample:

_____
_____

5) _____

How to sample:

_____
_____

6) _____

How to sample:

_____
_____

7) _____

How to sample:

_____
_____

8) _____

How to sample:

_____
_____

9) _____

How to sample:

_____
_____

10) _____

How to sample:

_____

_____

What I've covered in this chapter is really at the heart of leading you to the right staircase… of helping you choose the main ingredient that suits you. Whether you are concluding your secondary education and making a decision about your college major or are completing your degree and ready to move forward in your career, now is the critical time to get this right. Go back and reread all or as much of it as you need to.

Having said that, the part you have to get correct right now is a pretty broad target. Again, it's the main ingredient. You will always have time to tweak the spices or continue to step along your staircase as things change and evolve.

The Process: Identifying Your Ingredients

Chapter Six:
Creating Your Ultimate Recipe

Having now gone through the process and with a full (or at least a better) understanding of how your mind works and your own Human Operating System, it's time to actually create your recipe. You should know your main ingredient that leads you to the right staircase. If you still feel uncertain, I encourage you to go back and reread the previous chapter. Even if you think you know but aren't 100-percent sure, I'll say the same thing. Reread the previous chapter. The process is really at the heart of elevating yourself above having to choose from the kids' menu. By doing so, you are taking the first steps to *designing* the career and life you want rather than allowing it to simply happen.

With your main ingredient in mind, you've visited the magazine rack and have done that exercise, and you're clear about what intrigues you. You have a grasp on your desired lifestyle and ideal work environment. You have a really good sense about the spices you want to add, so it is time to create the recipe that is the right one for you. I won't say the perfect recipe because, as you've seen in the examples I've covered, your career may be somewhat dynamic and changing. My brother is the perfect example of that, growing in his career without having to change staircases. If you've done any cooking, you know that recipes can always be tweaked – a little more of this, a little less of that – to suit your own palate as it changes.

No Secret Recipes

Now, as recipes go, some people (perhaps even your mother or grandmother) are loathe to share them. They're family secrets, passed from one generation to another but never to be shared outside the family. Some cooks take pride in being asked to cook up one of their secret recipes, and they're happy to share the end result but never the actual recipe and proportion of ingredients. KFC is the classic example of a "secret" ingredient that sets them apart, and plenty of folks have tried (successfully or not) to uncover it.

That said, and I must be quite clear about your career recipe, there cannot be any secrets! **There are no secret career recipes.** You will do yourself a huge disservice if you fail to share yours. I want you to share your recipe with anyone who will listen. It is often in sharing your recipe that opportunity arises.

You have an idea of your path or staircase, so now what do you do? Where do you turn? How do you start? Before I ask you to actually create your recipe, I want to cover with you the critical reason to share it to help you go from concept to reality.

In my own case at the start of my journey, this happened when I shared with one of the families of an autistic child with whom I was working as a behavioral therapist. In my final semester of my master's program, one of the parents of a child I'd been working with for three years asked the seemingly innocuous question, "So, what's next for you?" It was an important question, and I knew I didn't want to be a family therapist, so I shared with her what I did want – my recipe: I wanted to work with individual minds in business. I was debating pursuing my PhD on the business side of psychology and trying to figure out my next step. Industrial organizational psychology was the item on the menu, but it still didn't quite include the right flavors I was seeking. As I shared this with her, a light bulb went off in her head. "It sounds like what you want to do is similar to a program that my husband is participating in. You should talk to him."

I shared my recipe with Ed, and he lined up a meeting with a company for which he was a client, and that was my introduction to the field. It was a coaching company that just happened to be looking for someone with a psychology background. They hired me as a coach with the intention of having me manage the coaching side of their program. If I hadn't shared my recipe, this would never have happened. Even if I happened to learn about this company, it would have been a much harder feat to land the job without my insider. You must share your recipe with anybody and everybody who will listen. You never know who they know or the connections they may have.

The adage "It's not what you know, it's who you know" could never ring truer. The more you share your recipe, the more these two things align for you. Others may have ideas about who you should be networking with and the contacts you should be trying to make.

Thomas Edison is known for his inventions and will forever be associated with the light bulb. However, he started his career sending telegraphs. Partially deaf, early Morse code was written, so Edison's handicap was not issue. However, technology advanced and sound became a necessary part of the transmission. Edison was now disadvantaged with fewer and fewer opportunities. At the suggestion of a friend (a.k.a. sharing his recipe and aspirations), he ventured to Boston which was at the time the hub of science in the country, and Edison reveled in it. Without this particular conversation, the inventions we appreciate today would probably have taken a very different path... although it's doubtful we'd still be in the dark.

Because sharing your recipe is such an important component to broadening your perspective about career and vocational possibilities, I want you to stop and think about who in your life right now can provide this broader perspective and connect you with a "who" to help you. List the name, how you are connected (e.g., relative, family friend, adviser, guidance counselor, employer, etc.) and the leads they may provide:

Name	Connection:	Lead Potential:

I've allowed space for a dozen names, and I strongly encourage you to think of *at least* that many people with whom you should share your recipe. If you can't come up with a dozen, ask some of the folks you have listed for their ideas. And don't feel you have to stop when you reach 12 names. The more the merrier!

Just remember: No secret recipes when it comes to designing and pursuing your career!

Sample Recipes

Just as your mother and grandmother wrote recipes on a card and filed them in a box (while you might opt to store them on a smartphone), here are some sample career recipes to help you solidify the concept.

Lauren's Recipe: *Mastering Minds for Success*
Main Ingredient: Psychology
Additional ingredients: Business, human behavior, high earning potential, autonomy, no location constraints, freedom of time, depth of work, helping a person move beyond where they are to achieve their dreams
Optional spices: variation of work
Putting it together:
I was looking for something that would allow me to work with the person working inside the business. Many of the fields at the time I started either focused on systems or simply leadership. I wanted the ability to guide/change/improve the human mind working in the business to improve outcomes. My hobby of home renovations underscores the same theme – seeing "diamonds in the rough" and shaping and polishing them into something desirable. My main ingredient has provided the opportunity

to transform human minds for the past 20+ years. I've not tired of it yet.

Craig's Recipe: *Enhancing Mechanical Performance*
Main Ingredient: Mechanics
Additional ingredients: aviation, earning potential w/ upward mobility, in-demand industry
Optional spices: ability to participate in training others
Putting it together:
Craig tinkered with everything right from the beginning. He took things apart to put them back together. He fixed cars, invented new tools, and worked on improving just about anything with an engine. His experience in the Navy introduced him to airplanes. He fixed those for a while. Each rung on his ladder moved him further up to where he discovered building airplane engines was his thing. He enjoys a successful career at GE earning a great living and fulfilling his recipe for success.

Anya's Recipe: *Architectural Design*
Main Ingredient: Design
Additional ingredients: artistic, mathematical, aesthetic, engaging with others, physical outcome of a product, familiarity with the building world, hands-on work
Optional spices: working directly with people (face-to-face)
Putting it together:
Anya is an extremely bright person, the kind of person who succeeds at just about anything she takes on. She earned a 4.6 in school, was a top-notch golfer, and very artistic. She needed the ability to combine her artistic side with her high

intelligence. Architecture became the obvious path and the perfect fit the moment we put these key ingredients together.

These three examples all use a different main ingredient, but it's important to keep in mind that countless dishes can spring from the same main ingredient – the chicken Parmesan vs. chicken Piccata example. Both use chicken but taste wildly different, and you might enjoy one and really dislike the other.

For example, I have a client who is pursuing a career somewhat similar to my own, using psychology as the main ingredient; however, that is where the similarity ends. While business is one of my additional ingredients, she has a strong focus on athletic performance. I'm quite happy to always work remotely, but she has a real desire to be face-to-face. If you fail to consider your additional ingredients and optional spices in building your recipe, you are severely limiting yourself and are effectively back to ordering from the kids' menu.

Take time now to develop your personal career success recipe. As you consider what goes into your recipe, bear in mind that each ingredient will have a varied level of potency. Just as with a cooking recipe, there are certain ingredients that would be great to have included but may not be required for the dish to still be tasty, while other ingredients must not be omitted. The same will be true for your own recipe. For the purposes of this exercise, include all of the ingredients on your wish list. We can worry about the exact makeup of your ingredients later. Start with the ideal.

Creating Your Ultimate Recipe

My Recipe: _____

Main Ingredient: _____

Additional ingredients:

_____
_____
_____
_____
_____
_____
_____
_____
_____
_____

Putting it together:

_____
_____
_____
_____
_____
_____
_____
_____
_____
_____
_____
_____
_____
_____

Chapter Seven:
Invest in Yourself: Moving Forward with Confidence

Now having gone through all of the exercises in the previous two chapters to help you simultaneously zero in on your recipe and achieve a broader perspective, there is one more exercise that I want you to complete: write a letter from your future self. Perhaps you thought I was going to say set your goals, and while this exercise is a bit of goal setting, this is quite a different approach.

Maybe you've already been through a goal-setting process (or many more than one) in your life to this point. Most people, when thinking about goals, project forward: "In the next five years, I will do the following…". While goal setting is always beneficial, there is a better way to go about the process, and that's where writing a letter from your future self comes into play.

In writing the letter, your perspective is one of looking back and reporting on **what you have already achieved**. There's the difference and the rub between goal setting and writing a letter from the future. The former tries to look forward; the latter looks back with certainty and shifts your mindset. It also creates a better awareness of yourself and your desires. Most importantly, it puts you on the path to actually manifesting your future and destiny by designing exactly how it might look. This may seem a little "out there" if you've never heard of this, and the more specific you can be, the better.

Invest in Yourself: Moving Forward with Confidence

To start, choose a date some years ahead, let's say five to ten, depending where you are in your life as you are reading this book. Consider where you are living and with whom. Imagine yourself in the career or vocation that reflects your main ingredient. Share from the future what your daily activities are, where you've traveled, and how you spend your leisure time. Don't ignore your emotions – how you envision feeling – as you write.

Here's an example:

Dear Future Self:

I know you put a lot of work and thought into determining the best career path, and let me tell you, now looking back five years, it was all worth it. Many of our sorority sisters are still struggling and bouncing from one job to another in search of the perfect one. I wake up every day and look forward to the day.

Right before graduation, our adviser turned me on to a writing position for an internet site that focused on hospitality reviews and the travel industry. That was enjoyable but served to open more doors, and as I built out my portfolio and clip sheets, I realized that I had the skills and experience to begin freelancing. You bet it was scary to give up a steady paycheck and the benefits, but (and forgive the cliché), I'm living the dream.

Still an early riser, I start early according to my own schedule and finish in the early afternoon. The rest of the day is mine to head out for a hike. Colorado suits perfectly for that, especially the Grand Junction area. There's not a lot of snow, and since I don't ski but love to hike, it's perfect. I found a great rental cabin, which is also perfect since I'm on the road for a few days at least once a month, so I don't have to worry about maintenance and upkeep. I do quite a lot of writing about travel and reviewing various destinations for several internet sites and magazines.

Don't get me wrong. It's not like I don't have a boss – I have several, actually. It's everyone who gives me an assignment, but I always stay ahead of the curve regarding deadlines, and that allows me to continually up my rates. The money is much better than I might have imagined when I began, and the freedom and opportunities to travel are the icing on the cake. Like I said, I am living my dream.

In writing your letter from your future self, include:
- What your career looks like and entails.
- Details about your daily work and home life.
- Your hobbies and how you spend free time.
- Financial status.
- Describe your surroundings (geographic location, home environment, etc.)
- Include who you spend time with (immediate and extended family, friends, coworkers, etc.)

Using this approach, looking back as if it has already happened, you will find that bigger things open up in your imagination. When you try to project forward from where you are today, you'll struggle or stay small because you are still limited by your own current perspective. I want you to dare to dream big!

Wrestle with a Stranger

You only know one you – and it's a skewed perception of who you are. It is wrought with insecurity, inexperience, and certainly a narrative about who you believe yourself to be. Huh? You may be asking, "Who I believe myself to be? What does that mean?" You see, we all have a belief about ourselves – who we think we are – who we feel we "should" be – what we think we deserve (or don't deserve), and so on. If not managed, this internal voice stands in the way of who you are today and where you want to go.

Though you may have daily conversations with yourself (I can bet on that), you are not very good at seeing through the existing conditioning of your mind that muddies the waters of your potential. That "should" voice gets in the way. Your "no way I could do that" conversation gets in the way. Even the voice that may have a false sense of confidence can mislead you down a path that ends in a dead end.

One of the most useful things you can do for your path to success is to "wrestle with a stranger." Ideally, that stranger is someone who has limited reference of your past and sees you for your potential. That person is a value that is hard to pay for but well worth the investment.

Another benefit of "wrestling with a stranger" is that, when you tap into the right path or direction, you gain a level of confidence that you might otherwise not achieve. When I'm working with a client, it's apparent to me and I can hear through our conversation when we've landed on something critical. It's easy for clients to miss it because they are wrapped up in their own stream of thoughts.

For example, I'm working with a client who is really feeling lost and stuck without any clear direction. She's looking at job opportunities simply for the sake of having a job. She had one opportunity that popped up and as we discussed it, I pointed out that it had nothing to do with what we'd been talking about. The one ingredient for her that was most pervasive was creativity. She was on the verge of taking a job as an administrative assistant in a financial firm where she stated that the task she was most excited about was ordering lunch. As soon as we played this out, it was obviously not the right staircase for her. She had another opportunity that was not as robust in terms of income – working part-time as an assistant to a fashion designer handling social media. This was the field for which she had the most passion, the one that excited her most. It was palpable each time I spoke to her that made it obvious from my perspective, but because she is "too close" to her own thoughts it was easy to dismiss (or miss altogether). Her magazine rack exercise led to a pile of fashion magazines. She didn't have a design degree (her degree was in history) so she wasn't sure how to make inroads in this particular field. Then, this opportunity popped up seemingly right in front of her. Was it coincidence or a result of her clarifying what she wanted enough to see it?

As we wrestled through this concept together, it was evident that this would put her on the right path and take her where she really wanted to go. Although it was only part-time, it would provide experience and open many more doors to opportunities that involved her critical ingredient – creativity. She realized that sticking with her main ingredient was much more important than a full-time job. After this poignant clarification, she created a list of people she knew in the industry who she could interview to gain more information and connections.

Here's something you might not realize: You've never seen the back of your own head. When I suggest that, people always stop me to tell me they have… they confidently argue that they have by using a mirror. Well, actually, you need two mirrors! Regardless, you are not actually seeing the back of your own head. You are only seeing a ***reflection*** of it; a double reflection at that. The concept of wrestling with a stranger is analogous to using mirrors to see how the back of your head appears to others. The stranger helps provide a reflection of what you can't see for yourself. You have one reality – your own. It is a limited reality, especially if you have yet to experience much in the world whether it be through trial and error, traveling to other places, experiencing other cultures or simply by living life at different age levels or in different decades. Wrestling with a stranger allows you to be shown different perspectives and fast forward your pace of development.

When Should I Wrestle with a Stranger?

As we've gotten to the end of this book, while I've tried through these typed words to be that stranger who can wrestle with you to help you solidify your recipe… or at least introduce you to the ingredients you have but may have overlooked or broadened your perspective about career possibilities, I realize that may not always be possible. I recognize that you are still filtering through your own reality as you read my words. Some of you may nail it by going through these exercises, while others may need additional help. Here are some clues that you may need to wrestle with a stranger:

- You're looking over the exercises you've completed and notes you've taken and are still unsure about your main ingredient.
- You have plenty of ingredients but you are unsure about how you might masterfully put them together to go from chicken fingers to chicken Parmesan.
- You're torn between main ingredients or between various staircases and need help determining the right selection for you.
- Or you have a sense about a fusion recipe but aren't certain that it will really be edible or successful.

This book is intended to help guide you, but you may find you need additional clarification or help in getting over the one-sided wall that you currently face. Consider, for a moment, what a one-sided wall really is. It is a wall that you face that can feel insurmountable or frustrating at least. A one-sided wall seems impossible to scale... until you do. Sometimes you just need a little assistance to help you get over it.

A well-trained stranger can be just what you need to pull things together, land on the unseen obvious, or provide you the confidence you need in order to take the leap.

It may require a small investment into yourself, but it will likely be most valuable. Considering the high cost of education, extending it by changing majors can be very expensive. Spending years of trial and error which may or may not lead you to the ideal path could lead to frustration or worse, damage to your self-confidence.

I am excited to report that it was the success of the process that the young adults I worked with experienced that encouraged me to write this book. They all left the process having clarity on their career direction, an understanding on how to leverage their network of contacts, and maybe most importantly, confidence in themselves.

If you know your main ingredient but are unsure about how to put your recipe together, talk to someone who is working in that field… who's already on your staircase. If working with a coach is not feasible for you, connect with upperclassmen in your field of study and you might both end up benefiting from an introspective wrestling match.

Finally, I truly hope that you can envision a delicious future for yourself and now have more of the pieces you need and a greater understanding of how you can create and design both the career and life you desire. No more ordering from the kids' menu. There is so much more to life than that!

Resources:

Ch. 1
Statistics:

http://borderzine.com/2013/03/college-students-tend-to-change-majors-when-they-find-the-one-they-really-love/

https://www.heri.ucla.edu/monographs/TheAmericanFreshman2016.pdf

https://nces.ed.gov/pubs2018/2018434.pdf

https://completecollege.org/data-dashboard/

https://www.valuepenguin.com/student-loans/average-cost-of-college

https://sf.freddiemac.com/articles/insights/homebuying-with-student-debt

https://money.usnews.com/investing/investing-101/articles/2018-07-23/9-charts-showing-why-you-should-invest-today

Ch. 3
The Untethered Soul: The Journey Beyond Yourself by Michael Singer

https://www.youtube.com/watch?v=LnGj7DUOsMg&feature=youtu.be

https://tim.blog/

https://fourhourworkweek.com/

https://tribeofmentors.com/

https://www.headspace.com/headspace-meditation-app

Ch. 4

How Stuff Works, "How Operating Systems Work" by Curt Franklin and Dave Coustan

The Hijacker, Overcome Self-Sabotaging Behavior, by Lauren Doyle

Journaling Question Ideas:

If I could dream up the most ideal life, what would it look like?

        Who would I be married to?
        What would I do for a living?
        Where would I live?

How do I feel my day went today?

        What did I learn?

What was the best thing that happened today?

What do I want to do more of/better tomorrow?

Who did I meet today who could positively impact my world?

Who should I meet this month who could positively impact my world?

If I were to act boldly today, what would I do?

What is the one goal I have that I want to advance today?

> How will I do so?

What mental message held me back today?

What did I witness about others today that I can learn from?

What did someone do today that I would not want to do myself?

What did someone do today, that I would want to do myself?

Why do I deserve to have the career I love?

What do I need to do in order to further my ability to have that career (or relationship, etc.)?

What challenge (frustration) did I encounter today?

> How did I handle it?
> What did I learn from it?
> How will I use that challenge to help me?

What emotions did I experience today?

> How did I manage them?

What emotion did I experience today that worked against me?

What emotion did I experience today that worked for me?

What people in my world make me feel like I can successfully conquer the world?

What people in my world make me feel small or inferior?

> What is it about that person that makes me feel this way?
>
> What do I need to do with this relationship, so I can accomplish all that I want to?

What successes did I have today?

> What positive message did it reinforce that will help me accomplish what I want to?

If nothing held me back – I had no limitations, what would I want to accomplish?

About the Author

Lauren Doyle has been helping professionals make more money and have more fun for the majority of her career as a business coach. Because her background is diverse and includes a master's degree in Marriage and Family Therapy, she has had the opportunity to help many of her clients' adult children navigate the daunting challenge of choosing careers they love and helping set them up for untold success. Her skillset is an unusual talent that allows her to connect with this younger audience and relate to them through her own personal successes.

This book was written for you because she wanted to codify what has helped her and her clients achieve a life and career by design. Maybe it's her love of puzzles that allows her to help her clients put together the challenging puzzle of choosing a career that will marry each client's unique talents with their enduring passions to cook up the perfect recipe for choosing a rewarding career that is ideal for them.

Her "outside the box" thinking she helps her clients and herself live fulfilling careers and lives. She truly practices what she preaches. The concepts she shares has allowed her to: live on the beach in San Diego, become a snowbird in her 30s spending half the year on a lake in Michigan and the other half in beautiful Sarasota, Florida. She has been able to do this while achieving financial freedom as a result of cooking up her own recipe of creating a national business coaching firm, buying and selling millions of dollars of real estate, and being a great mom and wife.

About the Author

Lauren sat in your place once and has uncovered the formula that will help you ultimately determine your ideally designed career and life. Her practical approach makes her style relatable and the steps easy to implement.

She has a passion for renovating all things to make them better. From countless properties to hundreds of lives and businesses, she seems to have mastered the art of putting the right pieces in place to create the desired experience.

In addition to this book, Lauren has also written *The Hijacker: Overcome Self-Sabotaging Behavior*, a book that takes a deeper dive into the impact of understanding Human Operating Systems.

Her psychology and business background gives her a unique perspective that is most helpful in writing the ultimate recipe for career success.

www.ingramcontent.com/pod-product-compliance
Lightning Source LLC
Chambersburg PA
CBHW070123100426
42744CB00010B/1906